OPPOSING
VIEWPOINTS®
SERIES

School Policies

Other Books of Related Interest:

Opposing Viewpoints Series
America's Youth
School Dress Codes
Students' Rights

Current Controversies Series
School Violence

At Issue Series
Bilingual Education
Charter Schools
Child Athletes
Computers and Education
Do Children Have Rights?
Home Schooling
How Can School Violence Be Prevented?
Religion and Education
School Shootings
Sex Education
Should College Athletes Receive Gifts?
Standardized Testing
Year-round Schools

"Congress shall make no law ... abridging the freedom of speech, or of the press."

First Amendment to the U.S. Constitution

The basic foundation of our democracy is the First Amendment guarantee of freedom of expression. The Opposing Viewpoints Series is dedicated to the concept of this basic freedom and the idea that it is more important to practice it than to enshrine it.

OPPOSING
VIEWPOINTS®
SERIES

School Policies

Jamuna Carroll, Book Editor

GREENHAVEN PRESS
An imprint of Thomson Gale, a part of The Thomson Corporation

THOMSON
™
GALE

Detroit • New York • San Francisco • New Haven, Conn. • Waterville, Maine • London

Christine Nasso, *Publisher*
Elizabeth Des Chenes, *Managing Editor*

© 2008 The Gale Group.

Star logo is a trademark and Gale and Greenhaven Press are registered trademarks used herein under license.

For more information, contact:
Greenhaven Press
27500 Drake Rd.
Farmington Hills, MI 48331-3535
Or you can visit our Internet site at http://www.gale.com

LIBRARY OF CONGRESS CATALOGING-IN-PUBLICATION DATA

School policies / Jamuna Carroll, book editor.
    p. cm. -- (Opposing viewpoints)
    Includes bibliographical references and index.
    ISBN 978-0-7377-3826-1 (hardcover)
    ISBN 978-0-7377-3827-8 (pbk.)
    1. School management and organization--United States--Juvenile literature.
    2. Students--Civil rights--United States--Juvenile literature. I. Carroll, Jamuna.
    LB3012.2.S36 2008
    371.2'07--dc22
                                                                2007037456

ISBN-10: 0-7377-3826-X (hardcover)
ISBN-10: 0-7377-3827-8 (pbk.)

Printed in the United States of America
10 9 8 7 6 5 4 3 2 1

Contents

Chapter 4: What School Policies Are Needed in the Future?

Why Consider Opposing Viewpoints?

> *"The only way in which a human being can make some approach to knowing the whole of a subject is by hearing what can be said about it by persons of every variety of opinion and studying all modes in which it can be looked at by every character of mind. No wise man ever acquired his wisdom in any mode but this."*
>
> John Stuart Mill

In our media-intensive culture it is not difficult to find differing opinions. Thousands of newspapers and magazines and dozens of radio and television talk shows resound with differing points of view. The difficulty lies in deciding which opinion to agree with and which "experts" seem the most credible. The more inundated we become with differing opinions and claims, the more essential it is to hone critical reading and thinking skills to evaluate these ideas. Opposing Viewpoints books address this problem directly by presenting stimulating debates that can be used to enhance and teach these skills. The varied opinions contained in each book examine many different aspects of a single issue. While examining these conveniently edited opposing views, readers can develop critical thinking skills such as the ability to compare and contrast authors' credibility, facts, argumentation styles, use of persuasive techniques, and other stylistic tools. In short, the Opposing Viewpoints series is an ideal way to attain the higher-level thinking and reading skills so essential in a culture of diverse and contradictory opinions.

In addition to providing a tool for critical thinking, Opposing Viewpoints books challenge readers to question their own strongly held opinions and assumptions. Most people form their opinions on the basis of upbringing, peer pressure, and personal, cultural, or professional bias. By reading carefully balanced opposing views, readers must directly confront new ideas as well as the opinions of those with whom they disagree. This is not to simplistically argue that everyone who reads opposing views will—or should—change his or her opinion. Instead, the series enhances readers' understanding of their own views by encouraging confrontation with opposing ideas. Careful examination of others' views can lead to the readers' understanding of the logical inconsistencies in their own opinions, perspective on why they hold an opinion, and the consideration of the possibility that their opinion requires further evaluation.

Evaluating Other Opinions

To ensure that this type of examination occurs, Opposing Viewpoints books present all types of opinions. Prominent spokespeople on different sides of each issue as well as well-known professionals from many disciplines challenge the reader. An additional goal of the series is to provide a forum for other, less known, or even unpopular viewpoints. The opinion of an ordinary person who has had to make the decision to cut off life support from a terminally ill relative, for example, may be just as valuable and provide just as much insight as a medical ethicist's professional opinion. The editors have two additional purposes in including these less known views. One, the editors encourage readers to respect others' opinions—even when not enhanced by professional credibility. It is only by reading or listening to and objectively evaluating others' ideas that one can determine whether they are worthy of consideration. Two, the inclusion of such viewpoints encourages the important critical thinking skill of objectively evaluating an author's credentials and bias. This evaluation will illuminate an author's reasons for taking a particular stance on an issue and will aid in readers' evaluation of the author's ideas.

It is our hope that these books will give readers a deeper understanding of the issues debated and an appreciation of the complexity of even seemingly simple issues when good and honest people disagree. This awareness is particularly important in a democratic society such as ours in which people enter into public debate to determine the common good. Those with whom one disagrees should not be regarded as enemies but rather as people whose views deserve careful examination and may shed light on one's own.

Thomas Jefferson once said that "difference of opinion leads to inquiry, and inquiry to truth." Jefferson, a broadly educated man, argued that "if a nation expects to be ignorant and free . . . it expects what never was and never will be." As individuals and as a nation, it is imperative that we consider the opinions of others and examine them with skill and discernment. The Opposing Viewpoints series is intended to help readers achieve this goal.

David L. Bender and Bruno Leone,
Founders

Introduction

"Too much latitude is given to religious students."

Ellen Johnson,
president of American Atheists

"Public schools should not be hostile to the religious rights of their students."

Rod Paige,
former Secretary of Education

Whether religion has a place in public schools was a thorny issue throughout the latter half of the twentieth century. The First Amendment makes clear that government can neither endorse nor prohibit the exercise of religion. Yet when it comes to religion in school, courts that meant to resolve uncertainty regarding the law have been so divided over where to draw the line that schools are often left without clear guidance. Indeed, there is wide discrepancy in school policies across the nation, with some attempting to preserve religious students' rights while others aim to protect students' rights to an education devoid of religious influence. With each new court case or legislation, schools must again adjust their policies pertaining to religion, extracurricular religious clubs, and religious speech.

Religion in public schools is perhaps most controversial when it comes to school prayer. *Engel v. Vitale*, a 1962 U.S. Supreme Court decision, formed an important precedent. The case arose in response to a New York schools requirement that students recite a prayer each morning written by the state Board of Regents. The Supreme Court determined that the prayer was created by government officials for the purpose of furthering religious beliefs, and in consequence, it violated the

Constitution's promise of separation between church and state. Speaking for the majority, Justice Hugo Black maintained,

> One of the greatest dangers to the freedom of the individual to worship in his own way lay in the Government's placing its official stamp of approval upon one particular kind of prayer or one particular form of religious services. . . . Government in this country, be it state or federal, is without power to prescribe by law any particular form of prayer.

Thus, a school board cannot mandate even a nonsectarian prayer.

In ensuing years, court cases built on *Engel*, with judges deciding that daily Bible reading, requiring schools to display the Ten Commandments, setting aside a moment of silence specifically for prayer, and allowing clergy to lead prayers at graduations were just as impermissible as classroom prayer. After several years of precedents limiting religious expression in schools, in 1984 Congress passed a law that offered protections to religious students. The Equal Access Act states that for public high schools to receive federal aid, they must not discriminate against extracurricular activities clubs based on religious or political views. Under this law, a school that allows one after-school club to meet on campus must allow *all* clubs to meet. Six years after its passage, the act was affirmed in *Board of Education of the Westside Community Schools v. Mergens*. A high school had prevented a Christian club from forming at school because it feared that assigning it a faculty sponsor (required for after-school clubs) would appear to endorse Christianity. The Supreme Court stated in its decision that allowing extracurricular groups to use public facilities and be overseen by an uninvolved school official is not considered endorsement of the group. Years later, the Equal Access Act would be used to justify the formation of even more controversial groups at schools, such as gay clubs and groups that discriminate against homosexual students.

While it had been established that neither school officials nor clergy invited by them could recite prayers at school-sponsored events, in 2000 *Santa Fe Independent School District v. Doe* addressed prayers led by students. In this case, a Texas school district permitted students to vote on whether to have prayers before school football games and to elect a student chaplain to lead them. The Supreme Court conceded that "nothing in the Constitution ... prohibits any public school student from voluntarily praying at any time before, during, or after the school day," but the Court deemed the invocations unconstitutional because they "are authorized by a government policy and take place on government property at government-sponsored school-related events." Furthermore, the Court contended, holding an election on the issue allowed the majority to determine the religious rights of the minority, which it found unlawful. In his delivery of the Court's opinion, Justice John Paul Stevens wrote, "This student election does nothing to protect minority views but rather places the students who hold such views at the mercy of the majority."

Following many conflicting court decisions, in 2003 the U.S. Department of Education revised its Guidance on Constitutionally Protected Prayer in Public Elementary and Secondary Schools. The new guidelines offer sweeping protections of student religious expression. For one thing, they safeguard speech at school as well as at school-sponsored functions such as commencements, assemblies, and athletic events. They also state that administrators may not restrict students' religious (or antireligious) speech if student speakers are selected by "genuinely neutral, evenhanded criteria" and students retain control over the content of their expression. In addition, schools that fail to comply with the guidelines risk losing federal funding.

Despite this apparent victory for religious conservatives, new cases continue to highlight the contentiousness of religion in public schools. *Newdow v. Congress of the United States,* for instance, alleged that an atheist student was harmed by hearing her teacher and peers recite the Pledge of Allegiance each day in class because it includes the phrase "under God." The court initially agreed, but on appeal the Supreme Court threw out the case on a technicality, leaving the issue unresolved. In a case centered on controversial speech, *Harper v. Poway Unified School District* (2006) established that a high school could suspend a student for wearing a shirt that expressed his religious belief that homosexuality is shameful and should be condemned. Even though the school allowed other students to express their tolerance of homosexuality, the Court of Appeals found, the school acted rightly in curbing the boy's expression because it violated the school's harassment policy. In 2007, however, the Supreme Court dismissed the case and the appeals court vacated its ruling, fueling confusion over what types of religious expression schools can restrict, if any.

It is challenging if not impossible for schools to introduce policies that resolve all competing concerns and desires of parents, students, and educators. Experts grapple with contentious school measures in *Opposing Viewpoints: School Policies*, which includes the following chapters: Are All School Policies Necessary and Effective? Do School Policies Ensure Students' Safety? Do School Policies Respect Students' Rights? What School Policies Are Needed in the Future? As the heated arguments signify, constitutionally ambiguous school policies are ubiquitous and generate debate from all directions.

CHAPTER 1

Are All School Policies Necessary and Effective?

Chapter Preface

In September 1999, sixteen-year-old Anthony Jodoin was killed when the pickup truck he was riding in with four teens was involved in a rollover accident. While this incident, sadly, was not an unusual event, it captured headlines in Greeley, Colorado, because the crash occurred while the students were speeding back from their lunch break to class at Greeley Central High. Recalling a similar accident that killed four students one year earlier, parents and school officials lamented that both crashes could have been prevented had students been confined to campus all day. In consequence, one week later all high schools in the district closed their campuses, barring students from leaving at any time without parental permission. Fences, gates, and extra hall monitors ensure students' compliance with the rules. Yet while many claim the closed campus policy was needed to prevent traffic accidents, class-ditching, and tardiness, some people offer evidence that keeping students on campus has disadvantages too. Like many debates over the effectiveness and necessity of certain school policies, there are strong arguments both for and against closed campus policies.

Advocates of closed campuses cite many reasons for their stance, most notably the protection of students. "I'm concerned about kids racing to and from lunch in the middle of the day," Greeley police officer Steve Duus reported to his town's newspaper, the *Tribune*. "We had at least a dozen accidents during the school lunch hours last year." Louis Abuso, another traffic officer, implies that closing the campus would save lives: "All we're trying to do is keep these kids alive. Having an open campus is not assisting in that idea." Another advantage of restricted campuses, according to some administrators, is the monitoring of entrances and exits, which helps schools keep track of students. The parent of one high schooler whose campus is closed explains, "I'm glad to know where my son is during the day." Furthermore, it prevents outsiders from slipping onto school grounds. Principal James Ferguson of Hinsdale Central High School informed a school publication that his closed campus policy "was designed not to keep students and teachers in, but rather to keep others out."

Some who are concerned about closed campus rules, however, believe they are unnecessary and ineffective. At closed campuses, they assert, students who do not get along must remain together at school all day no matter how much tension rises. Ben Washington, a high school junior whose campus recently closed states, "A closed campus causes more fights, people are in each other's faces more. . . . The school is more congested now." Forcing students to remain on campus for lunch has an effect on food service as well, according to junior Dec Tran: "Our cafeteria is so small, we don't even all fit into it. They run out of food pretty fast, too." Other students complain about the food quality and choices in their school cafeteria. While some want healthier options than their school provides, others prefer cheaper fast food that is not available. In addition, some parents and students suggest that a more effective campus policy would give teenagers the opportunity to demonstrate that they can leave and return to campus responsibly and safely.

School officials have many points to consider when evaluating the necessity and effectiveness of campus rules. The authors in the following chapter examine controversial policies such as zero tolerance rules and drug testing programs, in many cases engaging in debate between protecting students and honoring their rights.

> "Now this strategy [of drug testing] is available to any school that understands the devastation of drug use and is determined to push back."

Student Drug Testing Programs Deter Drug Use

Office of National Drug Control Policy

In this viewpoint, the Office of National Drug Control Policy (ONDCP) contends that random drug testing is an appropriate and effective response to the problem of rampant, destructive student drug use. Programs that test students who participate in competitive extracurricular activities, it insists, both prevent initial drug use and channel current users into treatment. Moreover, this drug testing strategy improves school safety, morale, and pride, in the ONDCP's view. ONDCP is the government agency that coordinates U.S. drug control programs.

As you read, consider the following questions:

1. In ONDCP's view, what is the greatest threat young people face?

2. What point does the agency make about tuberculosis and other communicable diseases?

Office of National Drug Control Policy, "Drugs and Testing: Looking at the Big Picture," *Strategies For Success: New Pathways to Drug Abuse Prevention*, vol. 1, no. 1, Fall-Winter 2006, pp. 14–15.

3. What statistics are provided by ONDCP to support its assertion that drug testing is affordable?

Imagine a surgeon turning down the opportunity to use a powerful medical procedure that is government-approved, affordable, available, easy to use, and potentially life-saving.

It makes no sense.

The same could be said about schools that pass up a promising new technique for combating the scourge of substance abuse: random student drug testing. As any good surgeon knows, better methods bring better results.

Parents and educators have a responsibility to keep young people safe from drug use. In recent years we have made solid, measurable progress toward that end. According to the latest national survey in the Monitoring the Future series, the proportion of 8th-, 10th-, and 12th-grade students combined who use illicit drugs continued to fall in 2006, the fifth consecutive year of decline for these age groups. Similarly, results of the 2005 Youth Risk Behavior Survey show that rates of current marijuana use among high school students have dropped from a peak of 26.7 percent in 1999 to 20.2 percent.

This is good news, to be sure, but hardly reason to drop our guard. Consider: In 2006, according to Monitoring the Future, a fifth (21 percent) of today's 8th graders, over a third (36 percent) of 10th graders, and about half (48 percent) of 12th graders in America had tried illegal drugs at some point in their lives. Proportions indicating past-year drug use were 15 percent, 29 percent, and 37 percent, respectively, for the same grade levels.

The Threats that Drugs Pose

Marijuana remains the greatest single drug threat facing our young people. Past-year marijuana use among 18- to 25-year-olds (the group with the highest drug-use rates) fell 6 percent from 2002 to 2005, according to the National Survey on Drug

Use and Health. And yet, despite reduced rates in this and other user categories, marijuana still ranks as the most commonly used of all illicit drugs, with a rate of 6 percent—14.6 million current users—for the U.S. population age 12 and older. This is particularly disturbing because marijuana use can lead to significant health, safety, social, and learning or behavioral problems, and kids are the most vulnerable to its damaging effects.

Adding more cause for concern is the emergence of new threats, such as prescription-drug abuse. Over the past decade, youth populations have more than tripled their non-medical use of prescription drugs. Nearly one in five teens has taken prescription medications to get "high," according to a recent study by the Partnership for a Drug-Free America.

Our task, then, is to keep forging ahead and working to defeat drug abuse wherever it should arise. And to do this, we need all the help we can get. It is vital that we make use of the best tools at our disposal to protect young people from a behavior that destroys bodies and minds, impedes academic performance, and creates barriers to success.

An Effective Tool

Drug testing is just such a tool. For decades, drug testing has been used effectively to help reduce drug use in the U.S. military and the nation's workforce. Now this strategy is available to any school that understands the devastation of drug use and is determined to push back. Many of our schools urgently need effective ways to reinforce their anti-drug efforts. A random drug testing program can help them.

In June 2002, the U.S. Supreme Court broadened the authority of public schools to test students for illegal drugs. The ruling allows random drug tests not just for student athletes, but for all middle and high school students participating in competitive extracurricular activities. School administrators,

A Study Proves the Effectiveness of School Drug Testing Policies

A recent study in Indiana schools by Joseph R. McKinney, J.D., Ed.D., Chair of the Department of Educational Leadership at Ball State University, demonstrates the effectiveness of student random drug testing. The question asked in the study was "Does the implementation of a random drug testing program result in a reduction of drug and alcohol use among high school students?" . . .

The study looked at high schools with random drug testing policies. Ninety-four high schools were identified. Of these schools, 83 high school principals responded to the survey. The principals were asked to contrast substance abuse activity during the 1999–2000 school year when drug testing policies were in effect with the 2000–2001 school year when schools were not permitted to use random drug testing. The results of the study are summarized below:

85% of the high school principals reported an increase in either drug usage or alcohol usage among their students after the drug testing program was stopped, compared to the 1999–00 school year (when they had a drug testing plan implemented).

80% reported an increase in illicit drug usage during the 2000–01 school year compared to the previous year.

59% reported an increase in alcohol usage during the 2000–01 school year compared to the previous year.

David G. Evans,
Information Kit About Random Drug Testing of Students,
Drug Free America Foundation, Inc. www.dfaf.org.

however, need to consult with their counsels about any additional state law requirements regarding student drug testing.

Scientists know that drug use can interfere with brain function, learning, and the ability to retain information. Any drug use at school disrupts the learning environment for all students. It spreads like a contagious disease from peer to peer and is, in this regard, nothing less than a public health threat. Schools routinely test for tuberculosis and other communicable diseases that jeopardize student health. Clearly, there is every reason to test for drugs as well.

It is important to understand that random student drug testing is not a panacea or an end in itself. Nor is it a substitute for other techniques or programs designed to reduce drug use by young people. Testing is only part of the solution and cannot do the job alone. For maximum effectiveness, it should be used in combination with other proven strategies in a comprehensive substance-abuse prevention and treatment program.

Many Benefits

Schools considering adding a testing program to their current prevention efforts will find reassurance in knowing drug testing can be done in a way that is compassionate and respectful of students' privacy, pride, and dignity. The purpose of testing, after all, is not to punish or stigmatize kids who use drugs. Rather, it is to prevent drug use in the first place, and to make sure users get the help they need before the disease of addiction can spread. Drug testing is also affordable. Discussions with individual schools indicate that, on average, a high school with 1,000 students will spend approximately $1,500 a year to test 70 students, or 10 percent of the pool of eligible students.

As the number of schools with testing programs grows, so does the body of evidence suggesting that random student drug testing can have beneficial effects on school morale. Students feel safer participating in an activity when they know their classmates are drug-free. As former drug users get and stay clean, they make healthier and better choices about how to spend leisure time, and they are more likely to engage in school activities. School pride and spirit increase as students, parents, and the school community become more involved in the school environment.

> *"Students used illicit drugs at virtually identical rates in schools that drug tested versus those that did not."*

Student Drug Testing Programs Are Ineffective and Harmful

National Organization for the Reform of Marijuana Laws

The National Organization for the Reform of Marijuana Laws (NORML) supports adults who wish to use marijuana responsibly and fights to end marijuana prohibition. In this viewpoint, NORML argues that random drug testing not only fails to deter students from using drugs, but causes them harm. According to the organization, youths who know they may be tested may turn to alcohol or more dangerous drugs that are harder to detect on tests or may drop out of extracurricular clubs that require drug tests. NORML charges that suspicionless drug testing is an invasion of privacy and unfairly requires students to prove their innocence.

As you read, consider the following questions:

1. What does Dr. Howard Taras say may happen to students who do not engage in healthy extracurricular activities?

National Organization for the Reform of Marijuana Laws, "Just Say No to Random Student Drug Testing." Reproduced by permission.-

2. In NORML's view, how much does it cost to implement random drug testing programs in schools?

3. According to a source quoted in the viewpoint, what factors are not indicated by the presence of a drug metabolite?

According to the [2003] findings of the only national study to assess the impact of student drug testing on a national basis [conducted by the University of Michigan]: "Drug testing, as practiced in recent years in American secondary schools, does not prevent or inhibit student drug use." Investigators collected data from 894 schools and 94,000 students, and concluded that at every grade level studied—8, 10, and 12—students used illicit drugs at virtually identical rates in schools that drug tested versus those that did not. The U.S. National Academy of Sciences further adds: "The preventive effects of drug testing have never been demonstrated. . . . There is as of yet no conclusive scientific evidence from properly controlled studies that [random] drug testing programs widely discourage drug use or encourage drug rehabilitation."

The Harms of Random Student Drug Testing

Studies have shown that students exhibit greater negative attitudes toward school in districts that have implemented random student drug testing. This is because random drug testing undermines the trust between pupils and staff in an educational setting, a consequence that may impact negatively on other aspects of students' educational work. Rather than presuming our school children innocent of illicit activity—as most of them are—suspicionless drug testing presumes them guilty until they prove themselves innocent. Is this the message we wish to send to our young people: that we don't trust them?

According to a 2005 report by Britain's distinguished Joseph Rowntree Foundation, a perverse and unintended conse-

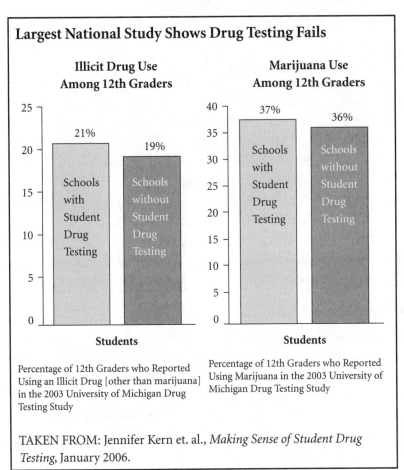

Largest National Study Shows Drug Testing Fails

Illicit Drug Use Among 12th Graders

Percentage of 12th Graders who Reported Using an Illicit Drug [other than marijuana] in the 2003 University of Michigan Drug Testing Study

Marijuana Use Among 12th Graders

Percentage of 12th Graders who Reported Using Marijuana in the 2003 University of Michigan Drug Testing Study

TAKEN FROM: Jennifer Kern et. al., *Making Sense of Student Drug Testing*, January 2006.

quence of random student drug testing is that it may "encourage some pupils to switch from the use of cannabis and other substances that can be traced a relatively long time after use, to drugs that are cleared from the body much more quickly," including alcohol and more dangerous drugs like cocaine and heroin.

Suspicionless drug testing targets primarily those students who are least likely to be using illicit drugs—those engaged in extracurricular activities—while at the same time creating a barrier for at-risk students who would benefit from participating in such activities, but may decline to do so out of fear of taking a drug test.

According to Dr. Howard Taras, chair of the Committee on School Health for the American Academy of Pediatrics, "[Random drug] screening may decrease involvement in extracurricular activities among students who regularly use or have once used drugs. Without such engagement in healthy activities, adolescents are more likely to drop out of school, become pregnant, join gangs, pursue substance abuse, and engage in other risky behavior." As a result, numerous health organizations—including the National Education Association, the American Public Health Association, the American Academy of Pediatrics, and the National Council on Alcoholism and Drug Dependence—oppose policies that would mandate randomly drug testing pupils who want to participate in afterschool programs.

Financial and Personal Costs

Random student drug testing programs policies often cost hundreds of thousands of dollars to implement, which is why they typically rely on federal funding. Instead of throwing taxpayer money toward this ineffective and unproven policy, why not use these funds to pay for school counselors and extracurricular and after school activities that we know will help keep our children healthy and safe?

Random student drug testing is a humiliating, invasive practice that runs contrary to the long-standing American principles of due process and presumption of innocence. It compels students to submit evidence against themselves and forfeit their privacy rights as a necessary requirement for public school attendance. Most teachers and school officials would balk at the idea of submitting to random drug testing and being forced to urinate on command before their supervisors. Why should our students be treated any differently?

Other Factors to Consider

Issues regarding drugs and alcohol should be between students and parents, not school officials. Schools are meant to educate, not police, our children. School officials are not surrogate parents, and issues regarding underage drinking or substance abuse are best left to be handled between parents and their children.

Urinalysis is not suitable for detecting drug impairment because the procedure only detects the presence of inert drug metabolites, not the presence of illicit drugs. According to the U.S. Department of Justice, the presence of a drug metabolite, even when confirmed, "does not indicate . . . recency, frequency, or amount of use; or impairment." In short, a positive test result tells parents and school officials, little if any substantive information, regarding pupils' illicit drug use habits.

Most schools reject random student drug testing. Ninety-five percent of schools nationwide do not randomly drug test their student athletes and only two percent of schools randomly drug test students who participate in extracurricular activities other than athletics.

| "Getting behaviour right in schools must be founded on an approach . . . that there are boundaries and that crossing those boundaries have consequences."

Zero Tolerance Policies Are Effective and Appropriate

Part I: Gerald N. Tirozzi; Part II: Department for Education and Skills

The authors of this two-part viewpoint advocate school zero tolerance policies, in which educators set clear rules, enforce them consistently, and expel students who refuse to obey them. In part I, Gerald N. Tirozzi, executive director of the National Association of Secondary School Principals, argues that administrators have a responsibility to develop policies that maintain safe, orderly, and drug-free schools. In part II, the United Kingdom Department for Education and Skills puts forth the opinions of Education Secretary Ruth Kelly, who asserts that disrespectful children must learn to take responsibility for their actions. She recommends that parents support schools' efforts to remove disruptive schoolchildren from classrooms, so that the remaining students can focus on learning.

Part I: Gerald N. Tirozzi, "Policies Are Appropriate," *USA Today*, January 2, 2004, p. 11A. Copyright © 2004 *USA Today*. Reproduced by permission; Part II: Department for Education and Skills, "Zero Tolerance to Indiscipline in Schools: Re-Drawing the Line," February 1, 2005. Reproduced by permission.

As you read, consider the following questions:

1. Why is it so difficult for educators to demonstrate that zero tolerance policies are working, according to Tirozzi?
2. What statistic does Kelly offer in support of her assertion that real progress has been made in tackling bad behavior?
3. In Kelly's view, what do every pupil and teacher have a right to expect?

Parents expect school leaders to provide their children not only a high-quality education, but also a safe and secure learning environment. Unfortunately, the drugs and violence that plague many communities sometimes penetrate our schools, causing outcomes that range from disruptive to tragic. This reality weighs heavily on school principals, who bear the daily responsibility to ensure the safety of their students and staff.

There is no magic solution to curbing violence or the sale of drugs in our society—let alone in our schools. Our elected officials regularly create laws meant to protect citizens from these acts and punish violators. In that context, zero-tolerance policies created by local school boards and personnel to deal with weapons, violence or drugs in school are altogether appropriate in the continuing effort to protect students and staff.

Creating Fair Zero-Tolerance Policies

However, as zero-tolerance policies are developed and implemented, several rules should be heeded:

- Engage parents and the entire school community in developing the policy. Clearly articulate the policy to staff, students and parents to mitigate misinterpretation.

- Fairly and consistently administer the policy. Ensure the punishment is age- or grade-appropriate and fits the "crime."

- Assure due process for accused students. Provide suspended or expelled students with alternative educational services and counseling.

- Ensure that disciplinary action taken against students with special needs is consistent with the provisions of the Individuals with Disabilities Education Act [UK law].

- Collect and analyze discipline data. Review the policy and practice annually.

Detractors of zero-tolerance policies point out well-publicized cases of unreasonably severe penalties for what some consider minor incidents. Supporters don't have it so easy. You won't see many news reports praising schools for an "uneventful" week. It is difficult to measure how often zero-tolerance policies prevented violence, drug traffic or a student from carrying a weapon into school. School leaders too often have been placed in a "damned if you do, damned if you don't" position over zero-tolerance policies. Media coverage of school-violence incidents raised community concerns across the country that produced calls for stricter safety guidelines. Yet the media and many in the community also often denounce school leaders for enforcing those policies.

It's true that imperfect policies sometimes result in excessive penalties, and those cases should guide policy revisions. But those cases are few and do not remove the need for a clearly defined policy designed to protect students and staff.

Principals always should err on the side of student and staff safety. School leaders should not have to apologize for upholding their communities' expectations for safe, orderly and drug-free schools.

Part II

Education Secretary [of the United Kingdom] Ruth Kelly today [February 1, 2005] underlined her support for schools to take a zero tolerance approach in tackling classroom disruption caused by a minority of pupils.

Mrs Kelly said that real progress had been made in tackling serious bad behaviour in schools, with permanent exclusions 25% lower than 1997, and pupil behaviour good in most schools most of the time. However, a focus was also needed on the disruptive behaviour by a minority of pupils that can prevent teachers from teaching and pupils from learning.

Components of a Zero-Tolerance Plan

A minority of schools also required additional support in rigorously enforcing clear, consistent discipline codes that were understood and supported by pupils and parents. And while parents had a right to expect their child to learn in a safe, undisturbed environment, they also had a responsibility to support schools in tackling any misbehaviour from their child.

She said that getting behaviour right in schools must be founded on an approach which made it clear that there are boundaries and that crossing those boundaries have consequences—a zero tolerance approach, underpinned by:

- local authority directors to review schools where behaviour is rated as unsatisfactory by Ofsted [Office of Standards in Education], and to develop action plans to revamp their behaviour policies;

- Ofsted follow-up visits to every school where behaviour is rated as unsatisfactory within 12 months to check on progress and ensure that improvement is under way;

Zero-Tolerance Policies Are Generally Fair

We can count many, many more instances where we have seen far too lax discipline in our schools than we can count cases where the discipline administered was overly harsh and abusively punitive as some critics want to suggest.

In the end, those kids who receive less than firm, fair, and consistent discipline end up being taught that there are no consequences for inappropriate—and sometimes illegal—behavior as long as it occurs within grounds of . . . schools.

National School Safety and Security Services,
"Zero Tolerance." www.schoolsecurity.org.

- a new drive by local authorities to use Parenting Orders [court orders] to reinforce parents' responsibility for dealing with their child's bad behaviour; and

- schools pooling expertise in new Foundation Partnerships, with resources devolved to their control from the local authority, to enable them to buy shared in-school or off-site support to remove disruptive pupils from classrooms and nip their behaviour problems in the bud.

Managing Pupil Behaviour so Learning Can Flourish

Addressing an audience of Headteachers in Blackpool [England], she [Kelly] said:

"Behaviour is good in most schools most of the time. Often schools are the most secure and stable environment in the communities they serve. But any poor behaviour is too much and should not be tolerated. We need to re-draw the line on what is acceptable.

"Good schools already have a strong school ethos and a policy on behaviour that's respected by the whole school community because it's clear, consistent and rigorously applied. This approach must be in every school with any level of bad behaviour dealt with promptly and appropriately.

"Equally, pupils who lack respect for themselves, respect for their classmates and respect for their teachers need to be made to take responsibility for their own actions.

"Parents too must support the school's behaviour policy and not automatically assume, when their child is punished, that their child must be in the right and the school in the wrong. Where parents do not take responsibility for their child's unruly behaviour, then it is right that action is taken to ensure that they do, through Parenting Orders administered by the courts.

"Every pupil and every teacher has the right to expect a safe, secure and orderly classroom, so that teaching and learning can flourish."

Mrs Kelly set out her ambition to see every secondary school being part of a partnership to manage pupil behaviour by September 2007. In return, new admissions protocols for hard to place pupils—which are to be agreed by September this year for vulnerable pupil groups such as looked-after children—need not apply to excluded pupils until such time as schools have agreed arrangements with LEAs [local education authorities] for strengthening the support available to schools to deal with disruptive pupils. However she said that she remained prepared to consider legislation to ensure that admissions protocols are in place everywhere, once the support infrastructure is in place.

| "Zero tolerance has not increased the consistency of school discipline."

Zero Tolerance Policies Are Ineffective and Harsh

American Psychological Association Zero Tolerance Task Force

The American Psychological Association (APA) aims to improve health, education, and welfare through psychology. This viewpoint is excerpted from a report of the APA's Zero Tolerance Task Force. According to Russell Skiba and his co-researchers on the task force, school zero tolerance policies apply predetermined consequences for specific actions, regardless of the circumstances. Such policies, in the task force's opinion, fail to achieve the goal of increasing the consistency of discipline and do not take into account the developmental immaturity of young people. In fact, claims the task force, zero tolerance codes create a threatening climate, may be discriminatory, and refer students to the juvenile justice system for non-threatening offenses.

As you read, consider the following questions:

1. What are the five assumptions of zero tolerance policies that the report attempts to discredit?

American Psychological Association Zero Tolerance Task Force, "Are Zero Tolerance Policies Effective in the Schools? An Evidentiary Review and Recommendations," Zero Tolerance Task Force Report, February 1, 2006, pp. 1–15. Adapted with permission.

2. What explanation do the authors provide for what they call the disproportionate discipline of students of color?

3. According to the authors, what is the school-to-prison pipeline?

Since the early 1990s, the national discourse on school discipline has been dominated by the philosophy of zero tolerance [ZT]. Originally developed as an approach to drug enforcement, the term became widely adopted in schools in the early 1990s as a philosophy or policy that mandates the application of predetermined consequences, most often severe and punitive in nature, that are intended to be applied regardless of the seriousness of behavior, mitigating circumstances, or situational context. Such policies appear to be relatively widespread in America's schools, although the lack of a single definition of zero tolerance makes it difficult to estimate how prevalent such policies may be. In addition to universal goals of any school discipline approach, such as maintaining a safe school climate, zero tolerance policies assume that removing students who engage in disruptive behavior will deter others from disruption, and create an improved climate for those students who remain.

In an era of educational policy defined by accountability, it is appropriate and important to examine the extent to which any widely implemented philosophy, practice, or policy has demonstrated, through sound research, that it has contributed to furthering important educational goals. Thus the American Psychological Association, as part of its mission to advance health, education, and human welfare, commissioned the Zero Tolerance Task Force to examine the evidence concerning the effects of zero tolerance policies. The task force examined the assumptions that underlie zero tolerance policies and all data relevant to testing those assumptions in practice. In addition, due to concerns about the equity of school discipline, the task force synthesized the evidence regarding the effects of exclusionary discipline on students of color and students with disabilities. Finally, the Zero Tolerance Task Force examined research pertaining to the effects of zero tolerance policies with respect to child development [and] the relationship between education and the juvenile justice system. . . .

The following are the findings of the Zero Tolerance Task Force.

Key Assumptions

Have zero tolerance policies made schools safer and more effective in handling disciplinary issues? We examined the data concerning five key assumptions of zero tolerance policies. In general, data tended to contradict the presumptions made in applying a zero tolerance approach to maintaining school discipline and order:

School violence is at a serious level and increasing, thus necessitating forceful, no-nonsense strategies for violence prevention. Although violence and disruption are unacceptable in schools and are hence key concerns that must be continually addressed in education, the evidence does not support an assumption that violence in schools is out of control. Serious and deadly violence remains a relatively small proportion of school disruptions, and the data have consistently indicated that school violence and disruption have remained stable, or even decreased somewhat, since approximately 1985.

Through the provision of mandated punishment for certain offenses, zero tolerance increases the consistency of school discipline and thereby the clarity of the disciplinary message to students. Consistency, often defined as treatment integrity or fidelity, is indeed an important criterion in the implementation of any behavioral intervention. The evidence strongly suggests, however, that zero tolerance has not increased the consistency of school discipline. Rather, rates of suspension and expulsion vary widely across schools and school districts. Moreover, this variation appears to be due as much to characteristics of schools and school personnel as to the behavior or attitudes of students.

Removal of students who violate school rules will create a school climate more conducive to learning for those students who remain. A key assumption of zero tolerance policy is that the removal of disruptive students will result in a safer climate for others. Although the assumption is strongly intuitive, data on a number of indicators of school climate have shown the opposite effect, that is, that schools with higher rates of school suspension and expulsion appear to have *less* satisfactory ratings of school climate, less satisfactory school governance structures, and to spend a disproportionate amount of time on disciplinary matters. Perhaps more importantly, recent research indicates a negative relationship between the use of school suspension and expulsion and school-wide academic achievement, even when controlling for demographics such as socioeconomic status. Although such findings do not demonstrate causality, it becomes difficult to argue that zero tolerance creates more positive school climates when its use is associated with more negative achievement outcomes.

The swift and certain punishments of zero tolerance have a deterrent effect upon students, thus improving overall student behavior and discipline. The notion of deterring future misbehavior is central to the philosophy of zero tolerance, and the impact of any consequence on future behavior is the defining characteristic of effective punishment. Rather than reducing the likelihood of disruption however, school suspension in general appears to predict higher future rates of misbehavior and suspension among those students who are suspended. In the long term, school suspension and expulsion are moderately associated with a higher likelihood of school dropout and failure to graduate on time.

Parents overwhelmingly support the implementation of zero tolerance policies to ensure the safety of schools, and

students feel safer knowing that transgressions will be dealt with in no uncertain terms. The data regarding this assumption are mixed and inconclusive. Media accounts and some survey results suggest that parents and the community will react strongly in favor of increased disciplinary punishments if they fear that their children's safety is at stake. On the other hand, communities surrounding schools often react highly negatively if they perceive that students' right to an education is being threatened. Although some students appear to make use of suspension or expulsion as an opportunity to examine their own behavior, the available evidence also suggests that students in general regard school suspension and expulsion as ineffective and unfair.

Discriminatory Policies

What has been the impact of ZT on students of color and students with disabilities? Part of the appeal of zero tolerance policies has been that, by removing subjective influences or contextual factors from disciplinary decisions, such policies would be expected to be fairer to students traditionally over-represented in school disciplinary consequences. The evidence, however, does not support such an assumption. Rather, the disproportionate discipline of students of color continues to be a concern and may be increasing; over-representation in suspension and expulsion has been found consistently for African American students and less consistently for Latino students. The evidence shows that such disproportionality is not due entirely to economic disadvantage, nor is there any data supporting the assumption that African American students exhibit higher rates of disruption or violence that would warrant higher rates of discipline. Rather, African American students may be disciplined more severely for less serious or more subjective reasons. Emerging professional opinion and qualitative research findings suggest that the disproportionate discipline of students of color may be due to lack of teacher

Recommendations to Reform Zero Tolerance Policies

Apply zero tolerance policies with greater flexibility, taking context and the expertise of teachers and school administrators into account.

Teachers and other professional staff who have regular contact with students on a personal level should be the first line of communication with parents and caregivers regarding disciplinary incidents.

Define all infractions, whether major or minor, carefully, and train all staff in appropriate means of handling each infraction.

Evaluate all school discipline or school violence prevention strategies to ensure that all disciplinary interventions, programs, or strategies are truly impacting student behavior and school safety.

Reserve zero tolerance disciplinary removals for only the most serious and severe of disruptive behaviors.

American Psychological Association Zero Tolerance Task Force,
Are Zero Tolerance Policies Effective in the Schools?
An Evidentiary Review and Recommendations,
February 1, 2006.

preparation in classroom management or cultural competence. Although there are less data available, students with disabilities, especially those with emotional and behavioral disorders, appear to be suspended and expelled at rates disproportionate to their representation in the population. There is insufficient data available as yet to draw any conclusions about the causes of disciplinary disproportionality for students with disabilities.

Policies Ignore Developmental Immaturity

To what extent are zero tolerance policies developmentally appropriate as a psychological intervention, taking into account the developmental level of children and youth? In this section, the task force considered evidence relating to the developmental capacities of youth that are relevant to the use of punishment in school, focusing on research on adolescent development. Research relevant to juvenile offending has found extensive evidence of developmental immaturity. Particularly before the age of 15, adolescents appear to display psychosocial immaturity in at least four areas: poor resistance to peer influence, attitudes toward and perception of risk, future orientation, and impulse control. The case for psychosocial immaturity during adolescence is also supported by evidence from developmental neuroscience indicating that the brain structures of adolescents are less well-developed than previously thought. Developmental neuroscientists believe that if a particular structure of the brain is still immature, then the functions that it governs will also show immaturity; that is, adolescents may be expected to take greater risks and reason less adequately about the consequences of their behavior. Finally a growing body of developmental research indicates that certain characteristics of secondary schools often are at odds with the developmental challenges of adolescence, which include the need for close peer relationships, autonomy, support from adults other than one's parents, identity negotiation, and academic self-efficacy. Used inappropriately, zero tolerance policies can exacerbate both the normative challenges of early adolescence and the potential mismatch between the adolescent's developmental stage and the structure of secondary schools. There is no doubt that many incidents that result in disciplinary infractions at the secondary level are due to poor judgment on the part of the adolescent involved. But if that judgment is the result of developmental or neurological immaturity, and if the resulting behavior does not pose a threat to safety, it is reasonable to weigh the importance of a particular consequence against the long-term negative consequences of zero tolerance policies, especially when such lapses in judgment appear to be developmentally normative.

School-to-Prison Pipeline

How has zero tolerance affected the relationship between education and the juvenile justice system? There is evidence that the introduction of zero tolerance policies has affected the delicate balance between the educational and juvenile justice systems. Zero tolerance policies appear to have increased the use and reliance in schools on strategies such as security technology, security personnel, and profiling. Although there have been increased calls for the use of school security technology and school resource officers in the wake of publicized incidents of school homicide in the late 1990s, there is as yet virtually no empirical data examining the extent to which such programs result in safer schools or a more satisfactory school climate. . . .

The increased reliance on more severe consequences in response to student disruption has also resulted in an increase of referrals to the juvenile justice system for infractions that were once handled in school. The study of this phenomenon has been termed the *school-to-prison pipeline*. Research indicates that many schools appear to be using the juvenile justice system to a greater extent and, in a relatively large percentage of cases, the school-based infractions for which juvenile justice is called upon are not those that would generally be considered dangerous or threatening.

| "The question should be whether a science teacher who does not recognize that evolution is merely a theory . . . is really qualified to teach science."

Science Classes Need Disclaimers that Evolution Is Only a Theory

Christian Law Association

In this viewpoint, the Christian Law Association (CLA) advocates teaching that evolution—the idea that life originated by evolving from one species to another—is not scientific fact. New evidence, it avers, proves that evolution could not have occurred in the way that its theorist, Charles Darwin, proposed. The association further contends that including in the science curriculum alternate theories of the origin of life, including the notion that God created the world, is both appropriate and legal. CLA provides free legal aid to Christians and churches that are prevented from practicing their religion.

As you read, consider the following questions:

1. In CLA's view, why do educators and courts fight to prevent legitimate critique of Darwinism?

Christian Law Association, "Is Evolution Still a Viable Theory?" www.christianlaw.org. Reproduced by permission.

2. What did Charles Thaxton demonstrate in his groundbreaking book, according to the author?

3. In the association's opinion, why is it important for citizens to be actively involved in school board elections and policies?

M ore than two-thirds of Americans favor teaching both evolution and creation in public schools. Some surveys show that eighty percent or more of Americans believe that God was involved in creating the world and us. Given these numbers, it is amazing that anyone was surprised this summer [2005] when President George W. Bush, from his Crawford, Texas, ranch, endorsed the teaching in our nation's public schools of more than one theory regarding the origins of the universe and of life.

Is Evolution Still a Viable Theory?

Many states and local school districts are beginning to take another look at their science curriculum. Can a public school present the latest scientific theories refuting evolution without violating the First Amendment's prohibition on government-sponsored religious instruction? Courts have not yet definitively answered this question, but the simple answer, it seems, is "yes."

State and local school boards and school officials have broad discretion to determine the content of the public school curriculum. Approaches to teaching evolutionary theories vary greatly from region to region. There is a broad spectrum of approaches to this issue being considered by various states and localities.

Most states and school districts, unfortunately, continue to present evolution as an indisputable scientific fact, even though scientists themselves only consider it to be a theory. We must remember that Charles Darwin thought up this concept while sitting on a small island observing nature in the middle of the 19th century. Science has come a long way since then, and new scientific concepts do not always comport with Darwin's ideas. Even Darwin himself purportedly no longer believed in his own theory when he died.

Why then do educators and courts fight so hard to prevent any legitimate critique of Darwin's theory? The answer is simple: evolution is the only theory of how we got here on this planet that does not require a belief in God.

The emergence of new scientific evidence refuting evolution has caused great uncertainty among public school science teachers and school boards when planning their science curriculum. Lawsuits and threats of lawsuits cause teachers and school districts to back away from teaching the science of origins in any way that would permit criticism of evolution. Some believe that even teaching about the controversy surrounding the theory of evolution would be a violation of the Establishment Clause of the United States Constitution. In fact, however, there is much that science teachers can present in their classrooms about various scientific theories surrounding the origins of life that in no way crosses the constitutional line.

Good Science

The most important issue regarding the teaching of up-to-date evolutionary theories in public school classrooms should not be the legal one. Instead, the question should be whether a science teacher who does not recognize that evolution is merely a theory and not a scientifically proven fact is really qualified to teach science at all.

By any modern scientific measure, macroevolution, evolution from one species to another, is an unproven theory, not a fact. Indeed, there is much lively debate in scientific circles today about macroevolution, the "Big Bang" theory, and many other issues of origins. Students who are not taught scientific arguments that both support and refute the theory of evolution, particularly macroevolution, are simply not being given a good science education.

Good science would allow public school teachers to teach about Dr. Charles Thaxton, who has completed post-doctoral studies in the history of science at Harvard University and molecular biology at Brandeis University, and Dr. Michael Behe who teaches biochemistry and molecular biology at Lehigh University in Bethlehem, Pennsylvania. Dr. Thaxton was the first scientist to propose the theory of intelligent design as an alternative to evolution. A prominent atheistic scientist wrote the forward to Thaxton's groundbreaking book, *The Mystery of the Origin of Life*. Thaxton demonstrated that when scientists attempt to prove evolutionary theory, they are required to manipulate the building blocks of life in a manner that actually disproves evolution and points toward the need for an intelligent designer to be involved in the origins of life.

Behe's effective challenge to Darwinian theories is based on recent scientific data reported in his book, *Darwin's Black Box: The Biochemical Challenge to Evolution*. In this book, Behe spells out his theory of "irreducible complexity," noting, for example, that new scientific information about the biochemical cell structure demonstrates that species could not have evolved as Darwin theorized.

Neither Behe nor Thaxton ever mention creationism. They never suggest who or what may have been behind the intelligent design seen in the universe. Their theories support the thesis that some intelligent designer must be linked to the origin of life in much the same way as an intelligent designer is linked to the development of a computer program. Intelligent design, as suggested by these and other scientists, is a theory that is more compatible with religious views of creation, than it is with Darwinism. For this reason, proponents of the exclusive teaching of macroevolution as a fact are attempting to suggest that intelligent design is really just a back door way of getting religion into the public schools. However, proponents of freethinking in the field of science argue that public school children cannot be properly educated without learning the broad range of scientific theories. In fact, they contend that school children cannot be properly educated about these controversial issues unless all origin theories are taught objectively. Proponents who argue that public schools should teach intelligent design theories along with evolution believe that this approach is teaching good science, not religion. They argue that a sound education is based on intellectual fairness and not on the suppression of relevant evidence that does not support the current dominant theory of evolution.

Evolutionary scientists have not refuted the new scientific evidence presented by scientists such as Behe and Thaxton. Instead, most continue to blindly argue that teaching any theory other than evolution is teaching religion.

Teaching Alternative Theories

The United States Supreme Court has never mandated that Darwinism must be taught as fact rather than theory, nor have judges ever prohibited science teachers from teaching about scientific evidence disproving evolution. In fact, the Supreme Court has already indicated that it would approve of a science curriculum that would teach much more than evolution. In a 1987 case, the Supreme Court said: "Teaching a variety of scientific theories about the origins of humankind to schoolchildren might be validly done with the clear secular intent of enhancing the effectiveness of science instruction."

Congress has also endorsed teaching evolution in a more balanced manner. The Congressional Report, which accompanied President Bush's education initiative in the No Child Left Behind Act of 2001, said:

> Where topics are taught that may generate controversy (such as biological evolution), the curriculum should help students to understand the full range of scientific views that exist, why such topics may generate controversy, and how scientific discoveries can profoundly affect society.

Poor Science

The quandary exists when poor science—*with anti-God contempt and arrogance*—must insist it has all the answers. Good science is discovery. To slam shut the books and declare "end of lesson—let's all go home because we know how life began," is *brazenly ill-informed.* . . .

[According to a panel of scientists testifying for a subcommittee of the Kansas State Board of Education] Darwin's theory of evolution is biologically, genetically, mathematically, chemically, metaphysically and etc. "wildly" and "utterly impossible."

Connie Morris,
Kansas State Board of Education Newsletter,
June 16, 2005.

The record is clear that school boards may constitutionally permit public school teachers to teach the critical new theories scientists are developing based on emerging data in the field of science. The theory of intelligent design is an objective development in this field, based upon new scientific data and research. Intelligent design does not unconstitutionally bring God into the classroom. Students are free to independently determine whether they believe God, an alien, or something else provided the intelligence that triggered life's origin. Recent trends in the law support such honest intellectualism in science classes.

Some school boards already concede that evolution is only a theory. They have tried unsuccessfully to communicate this message to their students by printing disclaimers on science textbooks, but have been prevented from doing so by the courts. One disclaimer struck down by the courts simply read:

This textbook contains material on evolution. Evolution is a theory, not a fact, regarding the origin of living things. This material should be approached with an open mind, studied carefully, and critically considered.

Nevertheless, a court forced the school board to remove the disclaimer from textbooks, claiming that it violated the Establishment Clause because it sent a message of endorsement for those who opposed the teaching of evolution for religious purposes. Other cases involving mandating the teaching of intelligent design along with evolution continue in the court system.

Teaching Creationism

Although the Supreme Court permits teachers to present a variety of scientific theories about the origin of life, when it comes to the teaching of creation science, different rules come into play. Creation science may not be taught alongside evolution as an alternative scientific theory. The Supreme Court has held that Creationism may not be taught as science in the classroom because creation science is a religious belief. This does not mean that Creationism may not be taught at all, but only that it must be taught as religion, not science.

There are appropriate and constitutional places in a school curriculum where various religious viewpoints regarding the origins of life may be presented. So long as such religious material is taught in a neutral, objective and academic manner— i.e., presenting students with various cultural and religious theories without expressing approval or disapproval of any one in particular—the constitutional standards for teaching religion in school have been met.

Teacher Compliance with Curriculum Is Critical

There is one critical warning that must be mentioned in the current debate regarding teaching evolution in public schools. Teachers are always required to teach the curriculum mandated by the school board that employs them. Even if Congress and the courts agree that schools may teach intelligent design in schools, if a school board chooses not to include that material in the curriculum, teachers are obligated to follow the decisions of the local school board. In the absence of a legislative or judicial requirement that intelligent design be taught, local school boards maintain control over the curriculum, not classroom teachers.

Progressive school boards may permit teachers to include Intelligent Design or other material challenging evolution at their discretion. Some school boards already permit science teachers to choose their own curriculum material and to incorporate critiques of evolution where appropriate. Teachers, however, do not automatically have individual discretion to create their own science curriculum. For instance, if a school board policy requires the teaching of evolution as fact, the science teacher does not have discretion to ignore that policy and teach evolution only as a theory. If the school board requires the exclusive teaching of evolution, a teacher does not have discretion to teach alternative theories. A teacher who teaches material outside a school board established science curriculum should expect to be disciplined by the school board, and can also expect that a court will uphold the authority of the school board to enforce the teaching of its approved curriculum.

This is why it is so important for citizens to be active in school board elections and to monitor school board policies and decisions. Ultimately, it is the school board that sets school policy regarding the teaching of science and other educational issues. Christians must be actively involved in school board elections if they want to have input into these sorts of policies.

Student Freedom of Expression

It is important to remember that no matter what curriculum is mandated for a science class, students may constitutionally bring their own religious perspectives into the science class-room discussion. Students have a constitutional right to express their religious viewpoints in class. For example, it would be appropriate for students to choose topics or do class assignments analyzing which theories of origins best fit with current scientific evidence—whether those theories are secular or religious.

The United States Department of Education affirms this view. The 2003 Guidance on Constitutionally Protected Prayer in Public Elementary and Secondary Schools addresses the issue of class assignments as follows:

> Students may express their beliefs about religion in home-work, artwork, and other written and oral assignments free from discrimination based on the religious content of their submissions. Such home and classroom work should be judged by ordinary academic standards of substance and relevance and against other legitimate pedagogical concerns identified by the school.

Because state and local school officials have broad discretion to establish the public school curriculum, there is a great opportunity for Christians to influence what is taught in their local school district. Christians can elect school board members who are committed to teaching good science. Under the principle of academic freedom and excellence, Christians can lobby the school board for a curriculum that teaches more than one theory of origins and that permits teachers to present scientific information to students that refutes evolution.

Christians should promote the teaching of alternative theories for the origin of life as a matter of good science. This will prevent students from being indoctrinated into the unproven theory of macroevolution. Only then will children in public schools be free to weigh the scientific evidence in a neutral manner and choose for themselves whether to believe in creation, intelligent design, or evolution.

| "*Evolution is an exhaustively tested, highly substantiated explanation for the origin of biological diversity. It is not controversial.*"

Science Classes Do Not Need Disclaimers that Evolution Is Only a Theory

Selman v. Cobb County School District

In Selman v. Cobb County School District, *Jeffrey Selman and other parents challenged the inclusion of a disclaimer on their children's biology books that labeled evolution as a theory, not fact. This viewpoint is excerpted from an* amicus curiae, *or friend of the court, brief in the case filed by scientists and educators in support of Selman. According to the brief, evolution is a highly valid explanation of the origin of the diversity of life on Earth. Presenting evolution as merely a "hunch," the authors complain, undermines education and fails to promote critical thinking skills among science students. Efforts to discredit evolution, they argue, are part of a campaign by a small, religiously motivated fringe group that aims to unconstitutionally inject religion into the public school curriculum.*

Selman v. Cobb County School District, *Amicus Curiae of Colorado Citizens for Science et al. in Support of Plaintiffs*, U.S. District Court, Northern District of Georgia, Atlanta Division, November 15, 2004.

As you read, consider the following questions:

1. In the authors' view, what two errors does the biology book disclaimer contain?

2. What comparison do the authors make between the Cobb County disclaimer and the one struck down in *Freiler v. Tangipahoa Parish Board of Education*?

3. What are the authors' objections to the textbook *From Pandas to People*?

There is no scientific controversy over the validity of the evolutionary explanation of plant and animal diversity, which is the grand unifying concept of modern biology. Although some religious organizations insist that there is, and have recruited spokesmen with only colorable scientific credentials to claim that there is, the fact remains that evolution is the only scientifically valid explanation for the diversity of life. Although a thorough defense of evolution is not possible in a legal brief, amici [friends of the court; those providing testimony] wish to provide a concise refutation of the notion that evolution is controversial, or that there is scientific debate over it. It is not controversial, and no serious or reliable scientific criticism of the validity of evolution has yet been presented.

The Integrity of Science Education Must Be Protected

Amici Colorado Citizens for Science, Kansas Citizens for Science, Michigan Citizens for Science, Nebraska Religious Coalition for Science Education, New Mexico Coalition for Excellence in Science and Math Education, and Texas Citizens for Science, are groups of scientists, concerned citizens, religious leaders, businesspeople, parents and educators, who are committed to maintaining excellence in public school science classrooms in their home states. Because evolution is one of the central unifying ideas in science, and also one of the most evidentially well-supported of all scientific discoveries, these organizations are all committed to protecting evolution education from those who seek to either eliminate it entirely, or water it down by bringing in religious alternatives dressed in scientific-sounding language. Amici are concerned that tactics such as the Cobb County "disclaimer,"[1] if left unchecked, will undermine evolution education throughout the nation.

Amici agree with the plaintiffs that the disclaimer placed by the Cobb County School Board in biology textbooks hurts biology education in a way that appeases sectarian interests. Amici contend that a first-class science education provides students with vital, meaningful ways to understand the world around them and will provide Georgia with the skilled labor force needed to expand our technological economy. Protecting the integrity of science education will contribute directly to the future of our students, our quality of life, and to the prosperity of the state of Georgia. Further, our efforts in Georgia will help other states and nations to protect science education from the incorporation of dogma and pseudoscience. Many educators, including amici, are familiar with the average citizen's lack of education or training in evolutionary biology. Religious interest groups opposed to modern science take advantage of this ignorance to promulgate confusion, as they have done in the amicus curiae brief filed in support of the plaintiffs. We respectfully submit information that we hope will illuminate these attempts to confuse the court.

Evolution Is a Fact *and* a Theory

The disclaimer contains two errors: first, that evolution is "not a fact" and, second, that evolution is "regarding the origin of living things."

1. The disclaimer read: "This textbook contains material on evolution. Evolution is a theory, not a fact, regarding the origin of living things. This material should be approached with an open mind, studied carefully and critically considered."

Evolution is both a fact *and* a theory. Stephen Jay Gould [explains in] *Discover*, "Facts are the world's data. Theories are structures of ideas that explain and interpret facts."

The *fact* of evolution is that characteristics of populations of organisms change over time, producing biological diversity. *See generally* Carl Zimmer, *Evolution: The Triumph of An Idea*: "In discussing the truth of evolution, we should make a distinction . . . between the simple fact of evolution—defined as the genealogical connection among all earthly organisms, based on their descent from a common ancestor, and the history of any lineage as a process of descent with modification—and theories. . .that have been proposed to explain the causes of evolutionary change." The fact that organisms change over time, producing biological diversity, is undisputed, even by the public. The *theory* of evolution explains the fact of evolution, by identifying the mechanisms responsible for changes in populations. John Rennie [states in] *Scientific American*, "In addition to the *theory* of evolution, meaning the idea of descent with modification, one may also speak of the *fact* of evolution. . . . The fossil record and abundant other evidence testify that organisms have evolved through time. Although no one observed those transformations, the indirect evidence is clear, unambiguous and compelling."

These mechanisms include mutation, gene duplication, natural and sexual selection, migration, and genetic drift (not just mutation and selection as the Discovery Institute misleadingly suggests), and have been well tested, studied, and confirmed over the last century. Zimmer [writes,] "Evolution, the basic organizing concept of all the biological sciences, has been validated to an equally high degree, and therefore may be designated as true or factual."

There is no scientific controversy or debate about existence or utility of these mechanisms. [According to] Stephen Jay Gould and Richard Dawkins, [in] *Letter to the New York Review of Books*, "[N]o qualified scientist doubts that evolu-

Intelligent Design

Of course we want to discuss interesting new controversial ideas in science. Unfortunately, intelligent design isn't one. . . . In physics, there are hundreds if not thousands of articles on challenges to Newtonian gravity, ideas that Newtonian gravity changes on the scale of a galaxy. But I don't see people saying we should in high school physics classes not teach gravity.

There's an idea where people have actually tried to propose tests and make alternative theories that really make sense and people are actually exploring them. . . . But intelligent design hasn't even reached that. There are basically no scientific articles, no proposals, it hasn't affected the essential thinking of the way biology is performed and until it does, there's no reason to talk about it.

Lawrence Krauss in PBS Online News Hour, *"Intelligent Design," August 5, 2005.*

tion is a fact, in the ordinarily accepted sense in which it is a fact that the Earth orbits the Sun." There is healthy debate amongst biologists about the *relative contribution* of various mechanisms, but the overwhelming consensus is that evolution does occur and the theory of evolution explains it exceedingly well. [Writes] Rennie, "Evolutionary biologists passionately debate . . . how speciation happens, the rates of evolutionary change . . . and much more. . . . Acceptance of evolution as a factual occurrence and a guiding principle is nonetheless universal in biology."

What Evolution Explains

It is important to note what evolution is not. Evolution is *not* a grand explanation of the origin of everything. Many critics perceive that the theory of evolution covers everything from the origin of the universe to the origin of species. In reality, biological evolution only discusses the origin of the diversity of life, not the origin of the universe, galaxies, solar systems, and not the origin of life. Although terms such as "stellar evolution" and "chemical evolution" are sometimes used, they are distinct from (biological) evolution and the theory of evolution. Evolution is concerned with the origin of the diversity of life, which can only occur after the origin of life. Therefore, any process leading up to the first life forms is not evolution, and not covered by evolutionary theory.

The placement of the disclaimer on biology textbooks unjustifiably encourages students to single out evolution as suspect, as if it were not a firmly established scientific fact. The disclaimer thus flatters misconceptions amongst students that a theory is a "guess" or a "hunch." This is the colloquial usage, but in science a theory is a well-substantiated explanation for observed phenomena. Good science education should equip students with critical thinking skills. However, such skills are wasted if students are encouraged to imagine that strongly established scientific theories are not really established. Students in secondary education are simply not educated enough about the biological literature to successfully examine the unifying concept of modern biology. As a result the disclaimer encourages unscientific thinking amongst students. As one scientist [Michael Ruse] puts it, "An indifferent purveying of wares is not education. One must offer children the best-sifted and most firmly grounded ideas that we have, together with the tools to move the inquiry forward."

In fact, the disclaimer is part of a coherent strategy to subvert evolution education. As several scientists have noted, defenders of creationist theories have devised a so-called "wedge strategy" to implement the teaching of non-scientific theories in the biology classroom. As one defender of evolution education [Dr. Eugenie Scott] puts it,

If someone were to charge that textbooks present atomic theory using evidence that is erroneous, misleading, and even fraudulent, and that we should therefore question whether matter is composed of atoms, eyebrows would be raised—at least at the accuser. . . . And if the same person proposed that citizens should encourage local school boards to insert anti-atomic theory disclaimers in science textbooks . . . and lobby state legislatures to restrict its teaching, it is doubtful that such exhortations would receive much attention. . . . Unlike atomic theory, evolution has obvious theological implications, and thus it has been the target of concerted opposition, even though the inference of common ancestry of living things is as basic to biology as atoms are to physics.

Indeed, like the disclaimer which the Fifth Circuit Court of Appeals struck clown in *Freiler v. Tangipahoa Parish Bd. of Educ.*, (2000), this disclaimer is designed to "impl[y] School Board approval of religious principles," and disapproval of the scientifically established principles of evolution. Thus "the disclaimer crafted by the School Board serves only to promote a religious alternative to evolution."

No Genuine Scientific Controversy

Concepts make their way into science education by first going through the process of science; this involves researching, publishing, defending, confirming, and earning consensus. Then educators decide if new concepts are suitable for the level of the students; this involves curriculum committees, government review, and finally official standards. However, there is no scientific support for supposed "evidence against evolution," and thus anti-evolutionists bypass this process and use politics to influence science education.

A popular political strategy amongst anti-evolutionists is to claim there exists a scientific controversy about evolution that students should learn about. Objective inspection of this claim, however, reveals that it is suspect. The claim relies on citations of popular press works by anti-evolutionists that are not part of the peer-reviewed scientific literature. When actual biological literature is cited, its conclusions are misstated or misunderstood. For example, the popular "intelligent design" textbook *From Pandas To People* (1989) includes a litany of basic, serious mischaracterizations of evolutionary science.

Another popular political tactic of anti-evolutionists is compiling lists of scientists who doubt evolution. These lists may look impressive at first, but in reality they contain very few biologists and virtually no one who has ever done scientific work on evolution. Despite claims that their ranks are swelling, the lists are stagnant at a few hundred signatures. In response, the National Center for Scientific Education (NCSE) has a growing list of over five hundred scientists, mostly biologists, who support evolution education. To show how many scientists support evolution education, NCSE includes on their list *only scientists named Steve* (or some derivation thereof), which is approximately about 1 percent of all scientists. At present, this list contains over 500 names. It is proposed that this corresponds to perhaps tens of thousands of individual scientists who agree that evolution is the proper scientific explanation that students ought to be taught. Moreover, the list of scientific and scholarly organizations that support evolution education is quite long. Within the biological and scientific communities, anti-evolutionists are an extremely minor, religiously motivated fringe group.

Infusing Religion into Education

Amici are gravely concerned about the many attempts by religious organizations to politicize the education of public school science students. Some groups, such as Answers in Genesis and the Creation Research Institute, are candid about their goal to eliminate what they sometimes call "evil-ution," and bring fundamentalist Christian doctrine into public school science classes. But other groups, such as Discovery Institute and IDNet, take pains to hide their agenda by cloaking it heavily in pseudoscientific garb.

These religious advocates are not engaged in quality science. Intelligent design activists, for example, have yet to publish any peer-reviewed scientific research supporting what they claim are scientific data showing the inadequacy of evolution to explain the diversity of life. Revealing their agenda, the Discovery Institute's president, Bruce Chapman, explained that the Center seeks "[t]o replace materialistic explanations with the theistic understanding that nature and human beings are created by God."

The bottom line is simple: evolution is an exhaustively tested, highly substantiated explanation for the origin of biological diversity. It is not controversial, although some religious groups have taken great pains to portray it as controversial. The Cobb County disclaimer is a part of a strategy which these groups have adopted in an attempt to undermine evolution education and replace it with a "theistic understanding" of the origins of species. Such an attempt is simply unconstitutional, since it is not the place of the state's schools to "aid one religion, aid all religions, or prefer one religion over another," according to [*Everson v. Board of Ed. of Ewing Tp.* (1947)].

Periodical Bibliography

The following articles have been selected to supplement the diverse views presented in this chapter.

Anti-Defamation League	"Religion in the Science Class?" 2002.
Peter Baker and Peter Slevin	"Bush Remarks on 'Intelligent Design' Theory Fuel Debate," *Washington Post*, August 3, 2005.
Suzanne Black	"Zero Tolerance for Wild Pupils? No, It's More like Zero Discipline . . ." February 11, 2005. www.thisisworcestershire.co.uk.
Economist	"Intelligent Design Rears Its Head," July 30, 2005.
Economist	"Life Is a Cup of Tea," October 8, 2005.
David G. Evans	"DSC Information Kit," 2002. www.student drugtesting.org.
Mark Fisher	"Zero Tolerance—For Mistakes or Second Chances," *Washington Post*, April 29, 2004.
Michael Howie	"Ban Violent Pupils, Urge Headteachers," *Scotsman*, November 21, 2005.
Richard Milner and Vittorio Maestro	"Intelligent Design?" *Natural History*, April 2002.
National School Safety and Security Services	"Zero Tolerance," 2007. www.schoolsecurity.org.
PBS Online NewsHour with Jim Lehrer	"Intelligent Design," August 5, 2005. www.pbs.org.
Jacob Sullum	"Let the Love Flow: Student Drug Testing," *Reason*, May 2004.
Ryoko Yamaguchi, Lloyd D. Johnston and Patrick M. O'Malley	"Relationship between Student Illicit Drug Use and School Drug-Testing Policies," *Journal of School Health*, April 2003.

CHAPTER 2

Do School Policies
Ensure Students' Safety?

Chapter Preface

In 2006, a pretty blonde girl enrolled at Falmouth High School in Massachusetts. Her mother had died, she told fellow students, and her father was away in the Navy. She asked nearly everyone if they could score some marijuana to help her deal with her troubles. Three months later nine teenage boys were under arrest for selling her marijuana thirty-one times and the drug "ecstasy" once. The girl was not a student but an undercover police officer.

Whether to allow undercover officers to infiltrate schools is just one of many decisions school administrators make to keep schools drug-free. Often the debate over how to keep schoolchildren safe causes conflict between people who feel that every measure must be taken to protect students from harm and those who feel that the benefits of implementing such rules do not outweigh the problems they cause.

Many administrators enact drastic measures to maintain order and catch troublemakers who jeopardize other students' safety. At Falmouth, for example, parents had complained that drug use was prevalent and kids were being exposed to it at school. There had also been a number of drug-related crimes around town. The mother of one student discussed the school's drug problem and the subsequent undercover operation with the *Cape Cod Times:* "We're glad they're taking a serious look at this and they're taking action." The police and school officials believed the sting would send a powerful message that the school is committed to halting drug use and would deter students from buying or selling drugs. The school's superintendent added, "Generally, the reaction's been very positive."

Besides, undercover operations are rare, states Tom Scott, executive director of the Massachusetts Association of School Superintendents. He informed the *Boston Globe*, "It's done where there are serious concerns and they need to go deeper into the scope of the problem ... [when] they don't have enough information. It is a decision made as a last resort."

Yet some people believe police do not typically belong in schools. For one thing, they claim, undercover stings destroy students' trust in school officials and police and breed suspicion among students. Eric Sterling, who helped draft federal drug laws in the 1980s, maintains in his blog,

> This trust-destroying raid may well disrupt the school environment more than the marijuana use that existed in the school. Every student feels betrayed and suspicious. Every new student will enter that school under a cloud of potential distrust for several years.

He wonders why the situation had not been handled with more wisdom and compassion. Parents of the accused students, for example, feel that sending a pretty girl with a sad story was unfair and may even constitute entrapment. As defense attorney Drew Segadelli puts it, "If a good-looking girl wants something, I would jump off the Bourne Bridge to help her." If drugs were a problem at the school, critics contend, any officer could have found dealers without having to play on young men's emotions. Some critics also point out that when police are sent to schools, minor infractions are criminally prosecuted rather than punished through the school. Students are more likely to be expelled or charged with criminal offenses than students at schools with fewer officers.

It is unlikely that school officials will soon agree on the best way to shield students from the harms of drugs. Agreement regarding the effectiveness of other policies meant to protect children, such as school surveillance and Internet filtering, is often just as difficult to reach. In the meantime, the long-term effects of such measures, including the drug stings at Falmouth, remain to be seen. The authors in chapter 2 address these school safety issues.

| "Our mobile screening program will send the message that attempts to bring weapons into our schools will not be tolerated and serve as a system wide deterrent."

Metal Detectors Maintain School Safety

Office of Mayor Michael R. Bloomberg

The following viewpoint is excerpted from a press release from the office of New York City mayor Michael R. Bloomberg. The mayor credits metal detectors for the recent reduction in crime in his city's schools. Scanning students, he asserts, caught at least 307 guns, knives, and other weapons in the 2005–2006 school year alone. Strengthening initiatives to include metal detector scanning on random days in more middle- and high schools will further bolster school safety, he maintains. In his view, such a program will force teens to reconsider bringing dangerous instruments to school.

Office of Mayor Michael R. Bloomberg, "Mayor Bloomberg, Schools Chancellor Klein and Police Commissioner Kelly Announce a New School Safety Initiative amid Significant Declines in Crime in City Impact Schools: Launch of Mobile 'Unannounced' Scanning Program Increases Breadth and Depth of School Safety Initiatives Citywide," April 13, 2006. www.nyc.gov.

As you read, consider the following questions:

1. Since the 2003–2004 school year, how much have major crime, violent crime, and total crime dropped, according to Michael Bloomberg?

2. What powerful message is being sent to parents, students, and staff, according to Chancellor Klein in the viewpoint?

3. What percent of weapons and dangerous instruments were discovered through scanning, in the author's opinion?

Mayor Michael R. Bloomberg, Schools Chancellor Joel I. Klein and Police Commissioner Raymond W. Kelly [of New York City on April 13, 2006] announced new school safety statistics that show significant gains in school safety Citywide. In the City's Impact Schools[1], statistics show a 59% decrease in major crime, a 43% decrease in violent crime, and a 33% decrease in overall crime. As a result, four schools will transition out of the Impact Schools program and two schools will be added—bringing the total number of Impact Schools to nine. In addition, schools previously removed from Impact status continue to show dramatic improvements in school safety. In schools citywide, major crime declined by 9% and violent crime dropped by 11% according to data for the 2005–06 school year through April 2. Since the 2003–04 school year, when the Impact program began, major crime in schools citywide has dropped 12%, violent crime has dropped 27% and total crime has dropped 7%. The Mayor also announced today the launch of a new school safety initiative that will bring mobile scanners to middle and high schools this spring to ensure that dangerous weapons are not brought into schools. The program will enable school safety officers to travel unannounced to schools across the City to scan for

1. Introduced by Mayor Bloomberg in 2004, the Impact Schools initiative aims to reduce violence by increasing security and police presence in schools.

Metal Detectors Benefit a Kentucky School

A day after Kentucky's East Carter High School used hand-held metal detectors to search students and staff members for weapons, Carter County Superintendent Larry Prichard reported that the searches had caused no major problems or delays.

East Carter High School is no stranger to violence. In 1993, a 17-year-old honor student brought a gun into his sixth-period English class and fatally shot his teacher and a custodian who'd come into the room to investigate. Taking no chances, Prichard said the metal detector searches would continue for the remainder of the [1998–1999] school year.

Students are required to line up outside the gymnasium doors to be searched before entering the building. Four city police officers conducted the searches the first day, but district officials said that school personnel would be trained to use the devices and would conduct the searches for the rest of the year.

According to Pamela Riley, executive director of North Carolina State University's Center for the Prevention of School Violence, hand-held metal detectors have become a fairly common tool for keeping weapons out of school buildings.

"Anecdotally, I know many assistant principals appreciate having these 'wands' on hand if there's a suspicion that a student might be carrying a gun," Riley said.

eSchool News,
"Keeping Schools Safe with Technology,"
www.eschoolnews.com, June 1, 1999.

weapons. The Mayor was joined by Deputy Mayor Dennis Walcott, Criminal Justice Coordinator John Feinblatt, Commanding Officer of the School Safety Division Assistant Chief

Gerald Nelson, NYPD [New York City Police Department] Community Affairs Bureau Chief Douglas Zeigler and Senior Counselor for School Intervention and Development Rose Albanese-DePinto for the announcement at Abraham Lincoln High School in Brooklyn.

Safe Schools

"Creating great schools also means providing a safe environment for learning," said Mayor Bloomberg. "The Impact Schools initiative has worked and crime continues to decline at these schools even after being removed from the Impact list. Now we'll build on what works. New and innovative safety initiatives like our mobile scanning program will send the message that attempts to bring weapons into our schools will not be tolerated and serve as a system wide deterrent to bringing contraband into schools. We won't allow a few people to destroy educational opportunities for others."

"Today's news sends a powerful message to parents, students and staff that our efforts to make schools safer are succeeding," Chancellor Klein said. "The citywide rates are clearly moving in the right direction and the Impact initiative is proving that even schools with long histories of disorder and crime can be turned around. Our continuing priority to provide every child with a secure place to learn will translate into rising achievement and a richer school experience."

"Police officers and school safety agents both are to be commended for helping to improve safety in and outside of schools throughout the city," said Commissioner Kelly.

Advantages of the Scanning Program

While overall incidents involving both weapons and dangerous instruments have fallen 4% so far this year, the number of illegal weapons confiscated has increased 5%. For that reason, programs to ensure that weapons do not get past the school door must not only be continued but strengthened. To further that goal, as part of the City's School Safety Initiative, a mobile scanning program will be implemented in middle schools and high schools across the City by April 26 [2006]. On random days, students at these schools will be asked to go through metal scanning machines similar to the ones used to screen airline passengers. These scanning devices can detect weapons and dangerous instruments such as firearms, knives and box cutters. These mobile scanning devices, deployed by the New York City Police Department (NYPD), will be temporarily installed in schools throughout the city without prior announcement. The unpredictable deployment of these scanning devices serves as a powerful deterrent to people who might carry illegal weapons into City schools.

In the last school year, close to 40% of all weapons and dangerous instruments were discovered through scanning. Currently, 21% of high schools and middle schools have scanning capacity. This year [2006], the number of scanning schools in the city has already increased 4%, from 79 to 82. Citywide this year, schools have confiscated 307 weapons (20 of which were guns)—up 5% from last year—and 1,355 dangerous instruments—down 6% compared to last year.

Posters informing students and the public of this process will be provided to all middle and high schools and prominently displayed inside the student and visitor entrance at all times. In addition, principals will send letters to all parents announcing this new policy. On the days that unannounced scanning is being implemented at a particular school, signs announcing the presence of scanning teams will be prominently posted outside of the school.

"Even as crime continues to fall throughout our school system, we cannot and will not rest on our laurels," said John Feinblatt. "When it comes to weapons, even one is too many. Thanks to the Mayor's new scanning program, students who are thinking about bringing a weapon to school will have to think twice."

Citywide Decline in School Crime

Through April 2, the number of major crimes in City schools fell 9% compared to last year with substantial declines in felony assault (down 21%) and robbery (down 11%). Overall violent crime fell 11%, driven not only by the decline in robbery and felony assault, but also by reductions in misdemeanor assault (down 7%) and sex offenses (down 22%). Although total crime this year is down by less than 1%, criminal mischief increased 56% largely due to a citywide crackdown on graffiti. Excluding the spike in criminal mischief, total crime citywide would be down 5%. At the start of the 2005—06 school year, the City increased the number of School Safety Agents (SSA) by 200 bringing the total number of SSA's to 4,625.

> "*[Metal detectors] make many students feel diminished and are wholly incompatible with the positive educational environment that children deserve.*"

Metal Detectors Create a Hostile Learning Environment

Elora Mukherjee

School metal detectors create an intimidating environment and detract from learning, according to the author of this viewpoint. Marvin M. Karpatkin Fellow Elora Mukherjee, writing for the American Civil Liberties Union (ACLU) and its New York State branch, the New York Civil Liberties Union (NYCLU), contends that scanning students with metal detectors delays them from class and unnecessarily intrudes upon their bodily space and property. Complicating matters, the detectors are managed not by educators but by police, who sometimes abuse their authority, arrest students for minor infractions, and confiscate harmless items like cell phones, the author maintains. The ACLU and NYCLU aim to defend the constitutional rights and liberties of all Americans.

Elora Mukherjee *Criminalizing the Classroom: The Over-Policing of New York City Schools,* New York Civil Liberties Union and American Civil Liberties Union, New York: NY: March 2007, pp. 6–9. Reproduced by permission.

As you read, consider the following questions:

1. How many Wadleigh students were late or absent from class on November 17, 2006, according to the author?

2. In the author's view, how many New York City students pass through detectors at their schools each day?

3. What was the administrators' solution to the hour-long scanning delays at DeWitt Clinton High, as the author puts it?

On the morning of November 17, 2006, the New York City Police Department (NYPD) swarmed Wadleigh Secondary School. The officers' descent on Wadleigh, a Manhattan public high school attended by over 880 students, was not a spontaneous response to an emergency situation. Instead, it was a routine, if unannounced, visit—part of New York City's campaign to reduce the number of weapons in schools by deploying NYPD personnel to a random junior high or high school each day to install metal detectors that students must pass through in order to get to class.

Chaos in the School

At Wadleigh, the NYPD installed metal detectors inside the school building before the school day began and sent in dozens of officers to patrol the school. Every student, in order to enter the building, was required to walk through the metal detectors and to have his or her backpack, jacket, and other belongings searched by officers' probing hands. Officers selected some students for additional scanning with handheld metal detectors, requiring them to lean against a table or wall, spread their legs, hold their arms out, and lift each foot to be wanded.

The officers did not limit their search to weapons and other illegal items. They confiscated cell phones, iPods, food, school supplies, and other personal items. Even students with very good reasons to carry a cell phone were given no exemption. A young girl with a pacemaker told an officer that she needed her cell phone in case of a medical emergency, but the phone was seized nonetheless.

The metal detectors and searches caused chaos with some students missing as many as three class periods while waiting in line to be scanned. In all over one-third of students were marked late for class. Attendance at Wadleigh dropped about ten percent that day.

Throughout the morning, police personnel hurled invective and threats at the students they were charged with protecting. Officers threatened students with arrest for refusing to turn over cell phones, for stepping out of line, and for refusing to be scanned. Officers cursed at students and scoffed at educators. When a student wandered out of line, officers screamed, "Get the f--- back in line!" When a school counselor asked the officers to refrain from cursing, one officer retorted, "I can do and say whatever I want," and continued, with her colleagues, to curse.

Carlos's Story

The threats of arrest turned out to be more than bluster. Several Wadleigh students were hauled to the 28th Police Precinct that morning for minor non-criminal, violations of school rules. Among them was Carlos, an eleventh grader and Vice-President of the School Government Association. Carlos, who worked thirty to forty hours each week after school and needed to communicate frequently with his mother about his whereabouts, did not want the police to confiscate his cell phone. When he became aware of the police activity in the school, he chose to remain outside in order to call his mother and ask her to pick up the phone, which she agreed to do.

As Carlos stood outside the school, a police officer approached and asked for identification. Carlos explained: "My mother's on the way. She should be just up the block. You can talk to her." In response, the officer said to a second officer, "What are we going to do with this smart aleck?" The second officer replied, "Take him to the precinct."

The officers handcuffed Carlos, seized his cell phone, forced him into a police vehicle, and took him to the precinct without informing school officials or his mother. At the precinct, Carlos was ordered to remove his belt and shoelaces and was forced into a cell.

Meanwhile, Carlos's mother—who did not find Carlos waiting for her when she arrived at the school to pick up his cell phone—began a frantic search for her child. Many phone calls later, she learned that Carlos had been arrested.

When she arrived at the precinct, officers returned Carlos's phone to her, but refused to release her son into her care. Carlos was released only after his mother had finally left the precinct. Upon his release, the officers issued him a summons threatening that if he did not appear in court, a warrant would be issued for his arrest. The charges were ultimately dropped.

What happened to Carlos and the other students at Wadleigh Secondary School on November 17 was not an aberration. In fact, this scenario takes place in New York City schools every day. Thousands of School Safety Agents (SSAs—unarmed employees of the NYPD School Safety Division) patrol city schools, alongside countless armed NYPD officers. And when the city's roving metal detector program descends on a junior high or high school, the number of officers present at that school multiplies.

Turning Schools into Juvenile Detention Facilities

Everyone wants New York City's students to be safe. The city has deployed large numbers of police personnel and adopted aggressive policing tactics in schools as a way of trying to create a safe educational environment for students and teachers. Unfortunately, however, these practices are frequently excessive and dysfunctional. . . .

New York City's school policing program makes many New York City schools feel more like juvenile detention facilities than learning environments. Every day, over 93,000 city children cannot get to classes without passing through a gauntlet of metal detectors, bag-searches, and pat-downs administered by police personnel who are inadequately trained, insufficiently supervised, and often belligerent, aggressive and disrespectful. Moreover, any middle school or high school without permanent metal detectors might—on any day—be unexpectedly forced to subject its students to mandatory scans and searches that would consume as much as three hours of class time. These types of police interventions create flashpoints for confrontations and divert students and teachers from invaluable classroom time. They make many students feel diminished and are wholly incompatible with the positive educational environment that children deserve.

None of this is necessary. Many educators believe that school safety should be the province of education officials—not the police—and that non-police strategies are needed to keep schools safe. Police personnel who are called upon to assist in schools must be properly trained and institutionally responsive to school administrators. If this were to occur, many of the excesses of the city's school policing program would be curtailed. If officers were instructed to intervene only when safety is at issue, rather than enforcing arbitrary rules regarding dress, food or educational materials that pose no safety risk, further abuses could be avoided. . . .

Time-Consuming and Expensive

In April 2006, the city reported that 21 percent of middle schools and high schools, 82 public schools in total, scan students using permanent metal detectors on a daily basis. The NYCLU's [New York Civil Liberties Union's] recent investigation revealed that students on even more campuses than these 82—at least 93,411 students attending at least 88 schools—

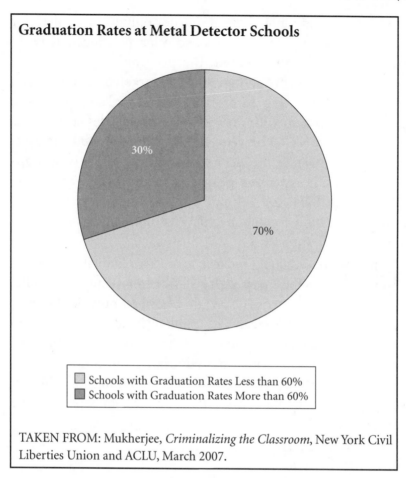

Graduation Rates at Metal Detector Schools

30%

70%

☐ Schools with Graduation Rates Less than 60%
■ Schools with Graduation Rates More than 60%

TAKEN FROM: Mukherjee, *Criminalizing the Classroom*, New York Civil Liberties Union and ACLU, March 2007.

must pass through permanent metal detectors to enter their school buildings each day. . . . [The] investigation was necessary because the city refused to disclose a list of schools with permanent metal detectors.

On April 13, 2006, Mayor [Michael] Bloomberg announced a further escalation of police activity throughout the school system, unveiling a program which subjects all middle school and high school students to NYPD-deployed "roving" metal detectors. The deployment of the scanners at any given school is unannounced, designed to catch students by surprise and to reduce the number of weapons in the school; it requires students at targeted schools to submit not only to metal detector scans but also to police searches and other policing activity. As soon as it was implemented, the program began to cause chaos and lost instructional time at targeted schools, each morning transforming an ordinary city school into a massive police encampment with dozens of police vehicles, as many as sixty SSAs and NYPD officers, and long lines of students waiting to pass through the detectors to get to class. It also appears to be an expensive program: in the fiscal year 2006–2007, which followed the mayor's announcement, the city's budget allocation for school safety equipment alone jumped 139 percent.

In November 2004, the New York City Council, concerned about school safety, passed legislation requiring the NYPD and the DOE [Department of Education] to provide the public with information regarding criminal incidents and certain non-criminal incidents in schools. Three months later in January 2005, the City Council passed a law requiring the NYPD to submit quarterly reports detailing the number of SSAs assigned to every public school. Both of these bills passed over the mayor's veto.

Students Protest

Community members have sought transparency and accountability in school policing, but with little success thus far. In July 2005, dozens of students and advocacy groups rallied at City Hall to protest the presence of armed police officers in schools and to urge the NYPD and the DOE to establish a way to allow students to help evaluate school safety personnel. The DOE and the NYPD ignored the protest.

In September of the same year, some 1,500 students from DeWitt Clinton High School in the Bronx marched nearly two miles to the local DOE office to protest police policies and practices that they said treated them like inmates and caused hour-long delays as the school's 4,600 students lined up to pass through metal detectors. Administrators met briefly with the protest organizers, but the only remedy they promised was to install more metal detectors to speed up the lines.

In August 2006, more than 100 students rallied at the DOE headquarters to protest the fact that policing practices in schools detracted from the learning environment and made them feel like criminals. To make their demands heard, the students delivered a report card on school safety to the Chancellor, and criticized the DOE for failing to respect students and listen to their concerns.

On November 16, 2006, students citywide made yet another attempt to reclaim their rights in school when about 800 students of the Urban Youth Collaborative announced a students' Bill of Rights. The Bill of Rights reflects a deep concern about the conduct of police personnel in schools, as evidenced by the inclusion of the right "to attend school in a safe, secure, non-threatening and respectful learning environment in which [students] are free from verbal and physical harassment, as well as from intrusions into their bodily space and belongings by school safety agents [and] police officers."

| "Iris recognition falls into the 'James Bond-ish' category of new technology being used to enhance school security."

Surveillance Technology Keeps Schools Secure

Rebecca Sausner

In this viewpoint, Rebecca Sausner asserts that school surveillance measures maintain student safety. Such measures, she says, include iris recognition systems, two-way communications systems, personal digital assistants such as Palm Pilots with student locator software, and a fortified safety officer force, among other things. Thanks to novel technologies, she maintains, school security directors can be made aware of activities occurring across their districts. Sausner adds that surveillance systems are considered so important to schools now that the need for them outweighs privacy concerns. She is a contributing editor of District Administration, *a magazine for administrators in kindergarten through high school education.*

As you read, consider the following questions:

1. In the author's view, what three ingredients are needed for safe schools?

Rebecca Sausner, "Seeing Is Believing: School Districts Are Using High-Tech, and Low-Tech, Approaches to Make Sure Students Are Safe," *District Administration*, vol. 39, no. 7, July 2003, pp. 36–39. Copyright © 2003 Professional Media Group LLC. Reproduced by permission.

2. What three technologies will be combined in the Spokane, Washington, district, according to Sausner?

3. How much funding does the author state that COPS has provided to hire additional officers?

When parents of students at New Egypt Elementary School in Plumsted Township, N.J., need to pick up their child for a doctor's appointment during the school day, many pause at the front door. They are prompted by a gentle, computerized voice and gaze upward into what may be the future of school security technology.

In just a few seconds, a wall-mounted camera takes a picture of the parent's iris—the colored ring surrounding the eye's pupil—and matches its 247 distinct points in the school's database of registered parents. If a match is found, the front door unlocks and the parent can proceed to the office to check in.

New Egypt's pilot program to test the iris-recognition access control system, used in tandem with a video camera-buzzer system operated by an office secretary, is perhaps the most advanced school-security technology installed today. And the nearly $300,000 price tag on the system, funded by a grant from the U.S. Department of Justice, is a new high-water mark at New Egypt in terms of security investments.

Increasing Threats to Student Safety

But school security experts and administrators across the country agree that as the demands of school security increase by the week, with fears of terrorism, bio-warfare and other attacks, technology is only one of the three main ingredients needed to create the safest schools possible. The other two—comprehensive written crisis plans and the invaluable boost in security that comes when adults develop positive relationships with students in their schools—aren't as sexy, or visible, but are perhaps more important.

"Today's school administrator faces safety threats ranging from daily issues of bullying and aggressive behaviors to potential extreme incidents of school shootings, sniper incidents and potentially being the target of terrorism," says Ken Trump, president of National School Safety and Security Services. "Every school administrator must be able to answer two questions: What steps did we take to reduce the risks of crime and violence, and how well prepared are we to manage those incidents which cannot be prevented?"

James Bond Technology

Iris recognition falls into the "James Bond-ish" category of new technology being used to enhance school security. But there are a whole host of more mundane devices that are being installed, or combined with existing systems, to give school security directors intimate knowledge of what's going on at any time, in any building, in the district.

The Spokane (Wash.) Public Schools, which have long been ahead of the curve when it comes to planning for school security, recently received voter approval for a $165 million bond measure that includes nearly $3 million for security upgrades at each of the district's 55 sites. The technological component of the plan calls for closed-circuit television cameras, new door and window alarm systems, and a card-swipe system that will allow staff to gain keyless entry into all facilities after hours. And while none of these systems alone are groundbreaking, Joe Madsen, director of safety, risk management, security and transportation, has a plan to tie all three systems together on the district's wide-area network. His vision is that if an alarm goes off at a building, school officials and local police will be able to go online and view which alarm is ringing, see the video from the cameras at that building, potentially hear audio from the building, and see which staff members have recently entered or left the facility. Staffers in thbuilding might have noticed something suspicious, for example, or be in danger themselves.

Effective Surveillance

Defined as "watch over someone or something," surveillance can be incorporated in two ways—actual and perceived. Crime is reduced as surveillance (or the perception) is increased. Surveillance components include:

- *Lighting*: Consideration must be given to where to place indoor and outdoor lighting and when to have lights turned on.

- *Landscape*: Good designs limit the opportunity for hidden or obstructed views.

- *Building layout*: The facility should provide views for maximum surveillance from as few control points as possible. Avoid circular or zigzag-shaped hallways.

- *Metal detectors*: These may add considerable time and expense as they control the access of students and visitors into schools. Economical mobile detectors providing random checks are an option.

- *Security cameras*: Systems can be expensive, but provide documentation for everything. These systems are helpful in cafeterias and kitchens, and can prevent questionable claims from employees. Security cameras are extremely effective when police have access to them.

Mark Lam,
American School & University,
September 1, 2005.

Some districts may go even farther than that. New Jersey-based Honeywell, known for its energy management technoleogy, is working with one district in Indiana to combine the security, fire alarms, heating and air conditioning systems—along with smart cards to be used for building access—for each of that district's 90 schools all onto one computer network. This type of system costs hundreds of thousands of dollars, but Honeywell prefers to discuss cost in terms of how much a district can save on energy and staff expenses.

"From a productivity and efficiency standpoint, we're freeing up the staff to do other tasks," says Greg Taylor, a security solutions specialist with Honeywell.

More Mundane Devices Are Beneficial, Too

On the other hand, some very good technology solutions can be bought relatively cheaply. Robert Bruce Campbell, superintendent of Pitman (N.J.) Public Schools, spent a total of $15,000 over two years to install cameras and intercoms along the main entryways of his district's five schools. "We try to do everything humanly possible to make the schools as safe as [we] can, without bankrupting the taxpayers," says Campbell, who speaks nationally about how to make school security cost-effective but still effective.

And while these systems help administrators deal with who, or what, may be in their buildings at any given time, other devices help manage student security. At Dr. Phillips High School in Orlando, Fla., some 3,800 students and a 65-acre campus directly abutting the Universal Studios theme park create a complex security environment.

Multi-Layered Communication

Assistant Principal Susan Averill uses golf carts, walkie-talkies, cell phones, pagers and the recent addition of Palm Pilots with TruSmart student locator software to cover the campus. The handheld devices hold not only student schedules, but also photographs and medical and contact information for each student. Locker combinations, license plate numbers, bus numbers, parking privileges, and other data can also be stored. Aside from helping staff to escort would-be class cutters back to their appropriate classes, the handheld student database would prove invaluable in a situation where buildings had to be evacuated and students accounted for, Averill says.

This multi-layered communication scheme is typical of a trend toward making communication capabilities a first priority in terms of security-related equipment purchases. This includes phones in classrooms, two-way public address systems, two-way radios, cell phones for crisis team members, and even charged bullhorns in the event of an emergency.

And while many of these technology investments provide both real and perceived security improvements, their effectiveness at this point is mostly anecdotal. In fact, the highlight of the New Egypt iris-recognition pilot project is not that the tiny district received such a large amount of money to invest in security. Rather, it's the adjacent $150,000 grant that went to an independent Maryland consultant to review the results of the project, for evaluation both by the Justice Department and the New Egypt school board. The report [became] . . . available [in 2003].[1]. . .

More Policing in Schools

A compelling public service announcement on TV these days preaches that parental involvement in teenagers' lives is the anti-drug; by the same logic, administrative and staff involvement with students may be one of the best antidotes to school violence, experts say. Administrators and teaching staff have known this for ages, but now many districts are supplementing this approach through adding school resource officers [SROs] to their security plan. The federal office of Community Oriented Policing Services [COPS] has funded more than 6,000 cops in schools since 1998, the year the program began, and recently announced another $20.5 million in funding for the hiring of additional officers, says Tim Quinn, chief of staff at COPS.

1. It found that both parents and teachers felt that the iris-recognition system is more secure and easier to use than the previous system.

"We have heard of a number of different [positive] results where situations have been averted, or a SRO has intervened in a situation that may have escalated because of the communication and the positive nature of the interaction" between students and cops in schools, says Quinn.

At Pitman, Campbell requires his building administrators to walk the grounds around their building each day and encourages all staff to be on the lookout for unusual events or potential intruders.

But no single tactic is the magic pill to increase school security.

"It cannot be just about the school security officer; he or she will not be able to do it all. It cannot be all about discipline," says Madsen. "Safe schools require the integration of building design, parking lot design, policies and procedures, relationships with students."

Cost and Need

Perhaps the two greatest political realities attached to school security is cost, which can run into the millions depending on district size, and the perceived need. The good news in the cost arena is that there are many federal grants available to fund security initiatives. But more importantly, parents and voters have come to realize, and even emphasize, the importance of school security.

"One of the compelling things that has changed is that security has gone from being a negative sell to becoming a requirement, very much like lighting and heating now," says Joe Zeigler, marketing communications manager at Honeywell.

The other issue is fear that schools will come to resemble prisons and students will feel like inmates.

"First and foremost, it's a school," says Madsen of Spokane. "It has to look like a school and feel like a school and education has to take place."

That said, many parents are willing to make sacrifices. Now, the perceived importance of security even trumps privacy concerns that would have taken center stage a few years back. In New Egypt, project organizers were expecting about 100 parents to volunteer to participate in the iris recognition program. In short order, they had more than 300 volunteers. Parents were heard commenting that they'd sacrifice just about anything to improve the safety of their kids, says Phil Meara, assistant superintendent.

"The hardest part of the whole security issue is to continue your vigilance even though nothing happens," Campbell says. "The biggest mistake we could ever make is thinking, 'It can't happen here.'"

| *"Who is more paranoid: the person who sees the need for all this security technology or the one who sees it as a form of totalitarianism?"*

School Surveillance Technology Is Totalitarian

Ronnie Casella

According to Ronnie Casella in this viewpoint, schools' use of scanners, closed-circuit televisions, biometric recognition, and other technologies encourages young people's complacency with widespread surveillance. Security corporations and government agencies, Casella maintains, create fears that schools and other institutions are dangerous in order to make surveillance technologies ubiquitous. This is worrying, he claims, because unrestrained surveillance teaches young people to readily relinquish their right to privacy and submit to unwarranted searches. Moreover, too much power is being given to the security industry, he warns. Casella has authored several books, including Selling Us the Fortress: The Promotion of Techno-Security Equipment for Schools.

Ronnie Casella, "The False Allure of Security Technologies," *Social Justice*, vol. 30, no. 3, Fall 2003, pp. 82–93. Copyright © 2003 Crime and Social Justice Associates. Reproduced by permission.

As you read, consider the following questions:

1. In the author's view, how many times a day is a person recorded on video surveillance in New York City?
2. What three things do security company ads aim to persuade individuals to allow, in Casella's opinion?
3. The author suggests federal agencies may be using schools to test security devices for what purposes?

The security industry trade magazine, *American School & University*, began an article about school safety with the following real-life scenario:

> As students were enjoying recess on the playground in the Plano Independent School District, Texas, a suspicious man sitting in a parked Cadillac tried to lure some of the children over to the car.
>
> When the teacher on duty saw what was happening and began to approach the car, the man drove off. That might have been the end of the incident, except that the teacher was carrying a two-way radio. She called back to the school office, and someone immediately called 911. A few minutes later, the man was in custody.
>
> "He was caught before he got out of the neighborhood," says Ken Bangs, director of police, security, and student safety for the Piano district. "Did we dodge a bullet? I believe that we did."
>
> For Bangs, it was more proof that the district's increasing use of radios was paying dividends in safer campuses, and more secure students and staff. "Having these radios makes a ton of difference," says Bangs.

Like many articles that appear in *American School & University, Security Technology & Design, Security Management*, and other trade magazines of the security industry, the use of technology is described as a boon for school safety, and the newest advances and improvements in technology are regularly featured in articles and represented in advertisements that appear in the magazines. In addition to radios, these technologies include metal detectors, scanners, closed-circuit televisions (CCTVs), iris recognition systems, and other forms of surveillance, detection, access control, and biometric equipment. Many of these items depend on technologies (such as digitalized networks and lasers) that were developed by military and security industry scientists beginning in the 1940s primarily for police and national security purposes during the Cold War. Today, the prevalence in high schools of what [author John] Devine called "techno-security" is an example of how these developments in technology have altered our public spaces, institutions, and homes. In the case of schools, the use of techno-security epitomizes fear of violence as well as fear of legal liability that convinces school district administrators that security technology is worth the expenditures. However, it also epitomizes the inroads that security businesses have made in the public school market. Peter Blouvelt, the executive director of the National Alliance for Safe Schools, remarked about security vendors: "Schools have become a major market for these guys. The proliferation of security equipment for schools has taken off."

A Surveillance Society

Schools are just one example of people's increased use and acceptance of security technologies in the United States. Government buildings, stores, offices, workplaces, recreation areas, streets, and homes have also been outfitted with CCTVs, biometric equipment, scanners, detectors, not to mention alarms, locks, and intercoms. At a security industry conference I attended as part of the research for this article, a spokesperson for a security corporation told conference participants that, according to research, in New York City an individual was likely to be caught on a security camera about seven times each day without knowing it; in London, the number was double that. Although the use of security technologies is often explained as a need during times of wanton violence and crime, the allure of technology and humans' fascination with gadgets and equipment partly explain why security technology is rapidly becoming a fixture in even the most idyllic areas. In the case of schools, though proponents of technologies warn against their misuse, they still believe that CCTVs, scanners, and other advanced technologies are essential for any overall school safety plan. Moreover, corporate incentives and federal support have made it possible for low-budget institutions and individuals to invest in security.

The mass installation of security technologies is one aspect of what [sociology professor David] Lyon referred to as a "surveillance society," whereby security items are at once ubiquitous and invisible. People accept them in public and private places and often acquiesce to the greater restrictions on their civil rights and privacy that ensue due to their use. [Media ecology professor Neil] Postman stated that in such a society, which he described as a technopoly, individuals find it almost impossible to think outside paradigms devoted to scientism, objectivity, and order. Critics of technology do not dismiss some key aspects (e.g., extending the lifespan of individuals and providing comfort), but they are skeptical of the promises made in the name of technology and its unrestrained use in society. . . .

Security Corporations Are Extremely Influential

Security corporations promote their products through donations and the free installation of security equipment in schools and in numerous other sites, including offices, restaurant chains, and recreation areas. Vanguard of Massachusetts offers free equipment and installation of technology that would ordinarily cost $40,000 to $300,000, depending on features. WorldNet Technologies in Seattle and AvalonRF in San Diego offer free installation of their product WeaponScan 80, an advanced metal (and plastic) detector that was originally developed by the Navy during the Cold War to track Soviet submarines. The most important benefit for corporations from these donations and pro bono work is the profit they receive from the monthly payments for upgrading and maintaining the equipment. Corporations also benefit from contractual clauses that allow them to feature the recipient of the equipment in their promotional materials and ads in trade magazines. WebEyeAlert includes in its ads news articles from the *Boston Business Journal* and the *Derry News* of New Hampshire on the schools that have received its web-CCTV monitoring system. This technology allows police officers to monitor students through CCTVs, modems, computers, and Internet networks.

An analysis of the ads allows one to understand their power in enticing school officials and others to invest in technologies. The WebEyeAlert pamphlet depicts various security markets and highlights the fact that security technologies are being introduced into almost all public and private places, including schools, homes, transportation stations, hospitals, cafeterias, and outdoor areas. The company also markets to municipal buildings, banks, malls, prisons, stores, and airports. At the center of the pamphlet is the picture of a school and a school bus. Another picture depicts a young couple proudly standing outside their home; young, upwardly mobile, good-looking professionals, they will probably have children and therefore have concerns about school safety, a connection that is made visually by the intersection of their image with that of the school. A picture of a hospital emergency entrance and ambulance also intersects with the school image, again drumming up concerns about safety for oneself and one's family. Visually connecting the image of the school to that of the po-

Illustration Instructing School Guards on Handheld Metal Detector Searches

TAKEN FROM: Mary W. Green, *The Appropriate and Effective Use of Security Technologies in U.S. Schools,* National Institute of Justice, September 1999.

lice officer in his cruiser is a white bubble. The officer shown is gaining visual access through the Internet to the "real-time video surveillance" cameras in the school. This ad encapsulates the security industry's widespread efforts to convince individuals and institutions of the alleged wisdom of investing in security devices.

Government and Security Companies Promote Technology

As noted, security corporations often donate security equipment and its installation in schools. Where does all the money come from to maintain and upgrade (and on occasions purchase) this equipment given schools' budgetary deficits? The answer lies largely in the financial support offered by the federal government for the research and commercialization of security technologies. Beginning in 2003, schools were identified as potential sites for terrorist attacks and the newly created U.S. Department of Homeland Security made funds available to schools to purchase security technology. This department appropriated over $350 million for, among other things, hiring high school police officers and buying security equipment through its Public Safety and Community Policing Grants. Other departments that offer funds for similar goals include the U.S. Department of the Treasury (through its Safe Schools Initiative, which also funds research conducted by the U.S. Secret Service), the U.S. Department of Education (through its Emergency Response and Crisis Management Grant Program and its Safe and Drug-Free Schools and Communities Act), and the U.S. Department of Justice. Schools are not the only ones to receive generous support. In 2001, all taxpayers began to benefit from a new tax code related to security. The Securing America Investment Act of 2001 (HR 2970), which amended the Internal Revenue Code of 1986, allows security devices in buildings and private homes to be considered an expense that is not chargeable to capital accounts; hence, security technology became a tax write-off.

Additionally, the "No Child Left Behind" law, [signed] . . . by President George W. Bush in 2002, provided funding for the School Security Technology Center (SSTC) at Sandia National Laboratories. Located in Albuquerque, New Mexico, Sandia employs more than 8,000 scientists, engineers, mathematicians, technicians, and support personnel; the laboratory was established in 1941 by the U.S. Department of Energy to support its nuclear weapons program. SSTC distributes information about school security and trains school employees to choose and use the right technology for their schools. In 1999, Mary Green, an SSTC employee, published *The Appropriate and Effective Use of Security Technologies in U.S. Schools* through the U.S. Department of Justice. It is considered one of the most comprehensive publications on the subject. SSTC is also involved in several security initiatives, including work with Albuquerque public schools to implement a system that uses hand geometry to identify parents and guardians of children. When parents or guardians register their children, they are assigned a personal identification number (PIN) and are asked to place their hand on a pad that uses biometric technology to record their hand features. Each time someone picks up a child at school, he or she enters the PIN and places a hand on the pad. If the PIN and the hand geometry match the information in the system, the person is allowed to take the child. . . .

The federal government's role in accelerating the use of security devices in U.S. society is demonstrated by the tax write-off for purchases of security devices, formation of the Department of Homeland Security, safe school grants, support of the Sandia National Laboratories, publications that promote advanced security technologies, and demonstrations of biometric security options for schools. Beyond that, security corporations and the federal government present a model of desirable behavior through the complacent, even pleased, people depicted in [brochures and advertisements]. Such ads ultimately seek to persuade individuals that they should allow themselves to be subject to routine searches, have their bodies measured and touched by lasers and scanners, and have information about them stored in databases—information that can then be shared with a greater range of federal organizations and police departments thanks to the USA Patriot Act of 2001.

Welcoming Security Technologies into One's Life

Beyond the federal support and corporate benefits and incentives stands the allure of technology and an almost myth-making quality to induce individuals to embrace the surveillance society in which they live. Corporate advertisers play on people's fears to promote technology as the way of the future and its increasing use as inevitable: "Take a closer look at the LG IrisAccess 3000—it's the look of things to come," claimed a 2002 advertisement by LG Electronics U.S.A., Inc., for an iris identification system. The president of Evolution Software, Inc., explained at a 2001 conference that "wearable security computer systems" would have technology "integrated in everyday life." She demonstrated a wearable computer equipped with voice recognition technology: a monocle strapped to her head (the computer screen), a little pouch on her hip (the computer), and a micro-keyboard attached to one hand; a hidden camera on her shoulder recorded her surroundings and could be projected on the monocle computer screen. Then she explained that the armed forces were interested in the "adoption of the technology for motion tracking systems and 3D augmented systems." Though the equipment makes one look part robot, the integration of technology with every-day life is a popular security industry item, a staple of security advertisements, and is commonly alluded to by school secu-rity dealers when they explain the "integration," "natural fit," or "harmony" between security technology and humans. . . .

Companies use this melding of humanity and techno-science to convince individuals to submit to devices and to ac-cept a world in which surveillance is common. When young people are asked to stand spread-legged at a school entrance or workers are asked to have their hand measurement taken before entering an office, the interaction between the overseer and the suspect depends on the compliance of the suspect. Compliance is achieved through the imposition of a codified authority (the presence of rules, policies, and laws), through actual punishment of transgressors, and by persuading indi-viduals that what is being asked of them is a natural part of life. . . .

The Agenda of the Power Elite

The power of the security industry has become concentrated in what [sociologist C. Wright] Mills referred to as a power elite, a group comprised of politicians, military officers, and corporate bosses.

The intentions of this power elite are only partly known. At some level, politicians who support the installation of se-curity equipment are concerned about the welfare of indi-viduals; yet, they are also interested in information gathering and in testing and using new products under development. Federal agencies may be using schools to test security equipment for later use by the military, for domestic policing and crowd control, or for information-gathering on young people, public housing occupants, those driving the highways, individuals who dress a certain way, or those who do not abide by all directives issued by the political establishment. Who is more paranoid: the person who sees the need for all this security technology or the one who sees it as a form of totalitarianism? Regardless of how one answers these questions, everyone should explore the purposes behind this security buildup and refuse to accept simple answers about safety and protection when there is little evidence that security technology actually makes us safer.

The longer a technology is used, the more entrenched in life it becomes. When technologies are new, or are used in newer ways (such as the application of satellite technology to cellular phones), their uses are easier to modify and their consequences easier to control. The use of security technology in public places in the form of biometrics, detectors, surveillance equipment, and advanced forms of access control are relatively recent developments. If we wish to question the unintended consequences of these developments, now is the time to do so. Too little is known about the consequences of the uncontrolled use of these technologies, yet most policymakers support them due to their allure and short-term promises of safety. If society becomes safer, if it becomes more difficult to smuggle weapons into schools, or if violence decreases, advocates of these technologies will claim that these are their intended consequences. However, if public and private institutions begin to resemble prisons, if new generations begin to accept unmitigated surveillance as a natural part of life, if people's civil rights become gradually revoked, or if people lose opportunities to develop human relationships, such consequences must be viewed as intended as well.

> *"Filters can shut down the browser or lock the computer when a user tries to access banned content, sending an alerting email."*

School Internet Filters Protect Children from Inappropriate Content

Becta

Becta (British Educational Communications and Technology Agency) is a United Kingdom organization that aims to improve learning through technology. In this viewpoint, Becta emphasizes that school Internet filters can be used in several ways to shield youngsters from unsuitable content. For example, the group explains, filters can block access to Web sites on a specific list or can allow students to access only preapproved sites. Some filters can screen incoming or outgoing e-mail, newsgroups, and chat, according to Becta. It further maintains that filters have safeguards against tampering by students and can be customized for different user groups and age levels to achieve the most appropriate level of security.

Becta, "How to Filter Internet Access in Schools," August 24, 2005. Reproduced by permission.

As you read, consider the following questions:

1. What does Becta say schools should consider when defining their requirements for a filtering system?

2. How do filters work when using a remote proxy system, according to the organization?

3. In Becta's view, what are the five actions by schools that any filter will require if they are to be effective?

Internet filtering systems prevent or block users' access to unsuitable material. When the filtering system is turned on, users cannot open or link to sites that the filtering system recognises as unsuitable. Many filtering systems will also provide facilities to filter incoming and outgoing email.

Filtering is an effective tool, but it is important to remember that no filtering software is foolproof and [it] should be combined with the full range of internet safety measures such as acceptable use policies, monitoring pupil activity, and education and awareness.

This document outlines some considerations for applying internet filtering in schools. . . .

How Do Internet Filtering Systems Work?

The most basic internet filtering systems have an 'allow' list of sites. Users can only access the list of sites supplied with, and supported by, the system. Access to all other sites is denied. This is the most restrictive type of filtering, providing limited access to the internet, and might take the form of a stand-alone web browser that only allows access to pre-screened safe sites.

Other systems have 'deny' lists, where users can access any site except those on the system's 'deny' list. These systems are much less restrictive, but the 'deny' list must be updated constantly to be effective, as sites and addresses often change.

Choosing an Internet Filtering System

There are a large number of filtering products available. Schools will need to examine filtering products and systems against their criteria to find the best match.

Most educational ISPs [Internet service providers] offer a filtered internet service. This can help prevent access to undesirable content, and can filter other services such as incoming and outgoing email. Additional software can be used in schools to supplement this service, and many filtering tools are also available for home users. The Becta Accreditation of Internet Services to Education scheme enables schools and other educational establishments to make an informed choice of ISP. The standards of assessment have been developed in consultation with partners in education and industry to ensure reliable and relevant information is provided. The accreditation process makes a technical assessment of filtering services provided by ISPs for factors such as browsing of web-based content, email filtering, blocking and filtering of newsgroups and chat services, and virus alerting. Assessments of service options such as customised filtering for different user groups are also made.

The following checklist may help schools to define their requirements:

- Identify requirements for a filtering system as accurately and as comprehensively as possible.

- Review current network infrastructure and internet connectivity to ensure that any solution will work with existing service.

- Consider where the filtering will be applied. There are a variety of locations from which filtering systems can be run, such as at individual PC [personal computer] level, at LAN [local area network] or proxy level, by the ISP or using a remote proxy server (see below).

For schools, services provided at the ISP or server level provide greater security and less chance of individuals tampering with settings, and are generally easier and more economical to manage.

- Consider when to filter. Different groups of users and machines may require different filters, and the importance of customisation facilities and the ease with which filtering systems can be administered and tailored to individual requirements needs to be considered.

- Consider if the filter can meet all of the school's requirements and, if not, how much customisation can be achieved. Of paramount importance at the client level is the ease with which the filter can be bypassed or disabled. The filter must be secure, especially on machines that are often used without supervision.

Schools will also need to consider how the filtering software actually manages attempted access to blocked resources or emails containing inappropriate language or material. For example, if a keyword matching/blocking system identifies a match, it might either not display the offending page or email at all, or display it but with the offending content obscured or stripped out. In extreme cases, filters can shut down the browser or lock the computer when a user tries to access banned content, sending an alerting email to the system administrator in the process. Find out exactly how the filter handles undesirable material and ensure that its methods fit with the requirements of the school.

An Educator Says Filters Are Necessary

I think legally it is in the best interests of schools to provide filtering. . . . Students can easily end up on sites that are not what you want an elementary child to view. Teachers can't hold every child's hand constantly. If students accidentally end up somewhere inappropriate, parents could blame the school for allowing their children to view the material. Schools open themselves up to lawsuits if they fail to provide some type of filtering.

That doesn't mean we shouldn't also educate children to do their own filtering. The ethical use of computers should be taught in elementary school and continually reinforced. Education is key to providing students with the skills they need to use computers and the Internet outside of the school setting. Many parents do not have filtering at home, but they want to be sure their child is not exposed to anything inappropriate at school. That is sort of a double standard, but that's the way it is. . . .

[In the filtering system we use,] if an educational site is blocked, teachers submit a written request to the principal asking that the site be unblocked. We unblock the site so the principal can review it. If he approves its use, we unblock the site for everyone. We have 280 teachers and 4,000 students using the filtering and, so far this year, we have had only two requests for sites to be unblocked. Both went through the procedure and both sites were unblocked. . . .

Most teachers are happy with the current system. Teachers can't be everywhere at once, and they don't have eyes in the backs of their heads. Most are relieved that some filtering is in place—for their protection as well as for the protection of their students.

Robin Smith, quoted in Linda Starr,
Education World, *June 4, 2003.*

Running Filtering Systems in Schools

Filtering systems can be installed and run from a variety of locations, ranging from a single user's PC to ISPs and beyond:

On individual PCs—A number of filtering tools are designed to run on stand-alone PCs. This approach may be appropriate for the home environment in that it allows parents to configure internet access as they choose. However, it is much less appropriate for deployment in schools across a network, as updates and reconfigurations will have to be carried out at each client machine rather than once centrally. Another disadvantage of such client-based filtering is that it may be possible for users to reconfigure or even disable the filter themselves, although many products include safeguards against such tampering.

At LAN or local proxy level—Here the filter is installed across a network so that it covers all clients on the network, intercepting all web page requests and email traffic. This means that all configurations and updates are carried out centrally making system administration and updating much easier. Such central installations are also harder for individuals to tamper with.

At the Internet Service Provider (ISP)—A number of ISPs provide services based around content specifically for children, alongside providing filtered internet access. Some will also restrict access to chat rooms, newsgroups or other types of Internet services as appropriate.

Using a remote proxy server—In this instance users configure their internet connectivity so that all internet traffic and requests pass through a proxy server. This server, which may be located geographically far from the institution's local area network, hosts the filtering or content access management system. Again this centralised approach is harder for users to tamper with.

Most web browsers provide some facilities to customise for security, privacy and content. These can be found in the help facility within the browser. Many search engines offer a filtering option which can vary from a simple setting of being either on or off, to offering different levels of filtering such as low, medium or high. The filtering options are not always easy to find and are usually located under 'Settings', 'Preferences' or 'Help' on the search engine website. . . .

Levels of Filtering

Different groups of users may require different levels of filtering. Schools may wish to provide younger users with more restricted access whilst allowing greater privileges to older users. Similarly, schools may require the filtering system to distinguish between different client machines on the network. Workstations in a more public location that are often used without supervision from school, college or library staff might need more restrictive filtering than workstations that are only used under supervision.

Levels of access supported by filters can vary greatly. Some filters are basically on or off whilst others allow specific configurations for different workstations at individual or group level.

Filters are far from being a "fit and forget" solution to the problem of preventing access to undesirable internet content. Any filter will require a degree of regular management, administration, maintenance, updating and review if they are to be effective. Schools should ensure that there is sufficient staff time, expertise and resources to manage and maintain any filtering solution.

Whilst devolving filtering responsibilities to a third party such as an ISP has advantages in terms of reducing system administration tasks, the trade-off is potentially reduced control over filtering methodologies. It is important to strike a balance between devolving responsibility and maintaining flexibility and control over what and how filtering is carried out.

Search Engines and Websites

Remember also that some search engines only return hits that are appropriate for children whilst some websites function as portals of links especially designed for children to explore. This method works by guiding users to appropriate content rather than by denying access to unsuitable materials. It is therefore somewhat removed from the more traditional approaches to filtering, but is still worth bearing in mind.

| *"One starts out meaning to filter dangerous or harmful material and ends up filtering substantive ideas. . . . Is this really what we want our schools to be doing?"*

School Internet Filters Are Ineffective

T.A. Callister Jr. and Nicholas C. Burbules

In this viewpoint, T.A. Callister Jr. and Nicholas C. Burbules argue that school Internet filters sometimes allow students to access inappropriate Web sites while also mistakenly blocking access to useful content. They claim that filters are antieducational and give educators a false sense of security, since the filters can be bypassed by students. Callister is an associate professor in the Department of Education of Whitman College in Walla Walla, Washington, and Burbules is a professor in the Department of Educational Policy Studies at the University of Illinois in Urbana-Champaign.

As you read, consider the following questions:

1. In the authors' opinion, who are filters actually designed to protect?

T.A. Callister Jr. and Nicholas C. Burbules, "Just Give It to Me Straight: A Case Against Filtering the Internet," *Phi Delta Kappan*, vol. 85, no. 9, May 2004, pp. 649–55. Copyright © 2004 Phi Delta Kappa International. Reproduced by permission.

2. What are five legitimate Web sites that the authors claim have been blocked by filters?

3. What point do Callister and Burbules make about commercial sites and Internet filters?

One of the most controversial and contentious issues surrounding the use of new information and communication technologies, especially in schools and libraries, is whether or not authorities should filter students' access to the Internet. On its face, the idea of filtering seems perfectly reasonable. Like other kinds of "filters," Internet filters keep out "bad" content while allowing "good" content to pass through. However, we argue that filtering is neither simple nor benign and that, with very few exceptions, schools and libraries should not filter students' access to the Internet.

We want to say up front that parents have every right to impose restrictions on what their own children view or do on the Internet at home, just as they have the right to limit what their children watch on television. Schools and libraries, on the other hand, have a wider educational responsibility to expose students to a broad range of ideas, experiences, and points of view, and what counts as educationally worthy is a matter for public deliberation. Some restrictions may be suitable in these contexts as well—young children, for example, can't check out certain books from the library. But Internet filters work in a different way: they are indiscriminate and often arbitrary, and they bypass public deliberation about what should and should not be filtered. The decisions are placed in the hands of unknown and unaccountable programmers, who develop their own criteria and automated procedures. From the standpoint of public education, this system inevitably leads to abuses and anti-educational effects.

What We Mean by "Protection" and "Harm"

Filtering policies are frequently justified by the admirable goal of "protecting" young people from "harm." Who could be against that? But such language is loaded, and the ideas of protection and harm need to be examined.

Because schools are generally thought to operate *in loco parentis* [in the place of a parent], it is easy, to transfer parents' impulses to use filters to protect their own children to the expectation that schools must do the same. But when we look at the situation through a different lens, it appears that protecting children may be less of a factor than protecting others in the educational realm. Filters are a way of protecting *teachers* from the upsetting nuisance of dealing with unpleasant or controversial topics in the classroom. They are also a way of protecting school *administrators* from angry phone calls (and even lawsuits) from parents concerned over occasional instances when students go to "bad" places on the Internet. Filters are a way for adults to avoid the hassle of dealing with instances of student misconduct, by attempting to forestall such acts. But in the process the vast majority of students, who would never abuse the system, are disadvantaged. Viewed in this light, the language of protection seems to refer most directly to the protection of adult interests.

The idea of filtering seems to imply protection from what may be harmful *coming in*. But filters are two-way operations: they block what comes in, but by that very action they also effectively block questions or inquiries from *going out*. Filters not only control the attempts of "dangerous" outsiders to reach an audience of young people, but they also restrict the attempts of young people to ask certain kinds of questions, to reach out and explore this new learning environment. How differently would we think about this issue if we said, "Filters are there to *control* students"?

Another loaded term is what students are being "protected" from—"harm." Filters prevent students from encountering things that are judged to be bad for them. But what harms are we talking about? Emotional distress? Corrupting influences? Encounters with people who would exploit children? These are hypothetically plausible, but worst-case, scenarios.

More commonly, what is judged "harmful" is what makes *adults* uncomfortable or what adults simply consider "inappropriate" for students. These judgments may or may not be justified, but the language—"protecting the young from harm"—shields such judgments from scrutiny. We all agree that we should keep children from things that could hurt them, but this agreement assumes what needs to be demonstrated. Is that which adults consider distasteful, offensive, controversial, or upsetting necessarily *harmful* to kids? Or does our categorizing things in this way simply mask the implicit value judgments being made? Where is the opportunity to question the educational price that is paid by erring on the side of excising Internet material that someone might consider "harmful," "offensive," or "inappropriate"? And what else is excised, inadvertently perhaps, that no one ever intended to filter out? How does filtering interfere with our goal of providing students with an education that is democratically open, intellectually challenging, and personally meaningful? In light of these concerns, we want to offer . . . reasons not to filter students' Internet access in school.

Filtering Software Blocks Useful Sites

Filtering software does not work in the way it is advertised. In one sense, we believe this consideration alone should end the debate. Filtering software too often blocks perfectly legitimate sites and often does not block the kinds of sites that it was intended to filter in the first place. There are hundreds of examples to be found on any number of anti-filtering sites on the Web. (Not surprisingly, many of these anti-filtering sites are blocked by filters, so even the opportunity to access points of view that might allow students to intelligently question filtering policies is stymied; this shows the vicious cycle of censorship such policies commit us to. Here, as elsewhere, technological solutions to one problem become an end in themselves and so eventually generate new problems.)

The Utah Education Network (UEN) is, according to its website, "a publicly funded consortium providing Internet access and supporting educational technology needs for Utah's public and higher education institutions, public libraries, and state agencies." The UEN is quite clear in stating that Utah schools must use filtering software. However, in a euphemism that should immediately make anyone more than a little wary, it refers to Internet filtering as "Internet Content Management." The software originally used by the UEN was SmartFilter. Sites that were deemed unacceptable (apparently determined by both human and computer analysis) fell into five broad categories: criminal skills, hate speech, drugs, gambling, and, of course, sex. The software also kept a log of each rejected request that listed the name of the requested site and the objectionable category into which it fell.

In 1998, the Censorware Project Organization—"censorware," not "content management," is the term preferred by anti-filtering advocates—after much resistance from UEN, was able to obtain the SmartFilter logs for 10 September through 10 October 1998. Here, from the Censorware Project Organization's report, are a few selected examples of items students and library patrons tried to get from the Internet but were blocked from seeing:

Under the category of criminal skills:

- the Krusty the Clown tribute page (from "The Simpsons");

- an e-zine (electronic magazine) about "modern Marxism";

- the Declaration of Independence; and

School Internet Filters Are a Form of Censorship

I worry that while preventing access to pornographic or unsafe materials is the reason given by those who advocate restricted access to the Internet in schools, the real motivation is political: keeping impressionable minds away from particular points of view. That is censorship at its most malignant. Even though CIPA [Children's Internet Protection Act] has taken the decision to use or not use Internet filters out of the hands of local decision makers, a strong commitment to intellectual freedom on the part of the school library media specialists, technologists, and administrators is not only possible, but even *more* important in a filtered environment.

Doug Johnson, "Intellectual Freedom and Internet Filters: Can We Have Both?" 2004. www.Doug-Johnson.com.

- the complete texts of famous works, including the Bible, *Moby-Dick*, The Book of Mormon, and *The Complete Adventures of Sherlock Holmes.*

Under the category of hate speech:

- www.hatewatch.org—the best-known anti-hate speech site on the Web.

Under the category of drugs:

- many sites discussing the debate over legalizing marijuana; and

- the Earth First! environmental group's website.

Under the category of gambling:

- the History of Nevada website; and

- the Instructional Systems Program at Florida State University (http://mailer.fsu.edu/wwager/ index_public.html)

Under the category of sex:

- the official "Baywatch" television show website;

- www.Birthcontrol.com;

- www.mormon.org; and

- dozens of news sites that included links to the Starr Report on President Bill Clinton and Monica Lewinsky [with whom he had an affair that led to his impeachment].

In Broward County, Florida, this same commercial software banned any sites having to do with vegetarianism or information on breast cancer.

How It Happened

Certainly, legitimate questions can be asked about the educational value of some of these sites (e.g., "Baywatch"). But the issue here is about unintended consequences: we intend to block X, but inadvertently block Y as well. How does www-.mormon.org get blocked for sex in Utah? How does the Declaration of Independence get blocked under the category criminal skills?

In some cases, we can figure out what happened. The Florida State Web address happens to include the letters w-a-g-e-r. The Declaration of Independence? The Sherlock Holmes stories? They are on the site wiretap.area.com, which contains the text of hundreds of books that are out of copyright, government and civics materials, religious materials, and so on. But this entire site was blocked. As to the others, we just don't know. SmartFilter, like most filtering software programs, keeps its lists of unacceptable sites—and its reasons for blocking them—private. This practice removes the judgments from public view and accountability. By the nature of the commercial (not educational) interests of these filters, they will always err on the side of blocking too much rather than too little.

Needless to say, a great deal is sacrificed when a young person cannot access information about [Karl] Marx, anti-hate speech, Sherlock Holmes, or the Declaration of Independence. Moreover, the general pattern of what gets "accidentally" blocked tends to have a biased, ideological effect itself—it isn't arbitrary or neutral. Sites that are in any way unconventional, controversial, or (by someone's standard) "radical" or "extreme" are more likely to get picked up by filters. Recall, for example, that the Declaration of Independence (like Marx) calls for citizens to violently overthrow their government if need be. And vegetarianism is considered "weird" by some people. Earth First! provides valuable information about environmental issues, but the organization does also advocate civil disobedience and acts of vandalism to protect the environment. Admittedly, there are parents and members of other groups who are perfectly happy to see these sites filtered, but this is not what the filtering software was intended for. In other cases, completely innocent sites are filtered simply because of key words that happen to appear on them or because of links they may have to other sites.

The overall impact of the filtering effort is to restrict access almost solely to mainstream, bland content that can't be construed as offensive to anyone. One starts out meaning to filter dangerous or harmful material and ends up filtering substantive ideas, information, and points of view. Is this really what we want our schools to be doing?

Allowing Access to Inappropriate Content

Although much of the discussion here and in the popular press has focused on examples of what is wrongly blocked, filters also fail in the other direction—that is, what doesn't get blocked. Out of curiosity—and in the context of writing this article—one of the authors set his Web search engine to its "family-friendly" (i.e., filtering) mode and typed in a crude synonym for breasts. The first site listed had a picture of just that. Or consider another example from a project designed to test filters: "One filter, at full settings, blocked a government brochure on the dangers of cocaine and let through a site describing in full detail how to make cocaine." Similar examples abound. Filters block too many things they should let through, and they let through things they are supposed to block. They simply don't work as advertised.

We also want to note, in passing, that few arguments about filtering ever discuss filtering "pop-up" ads or commercial sites, even though they usually have little educational value. Why isn't this an issue? Certainly, society realizes the tremendous power of marketing aimed at young people, but this is not seen as a serious potential "harm." Yet the fact is that the typical young person is far more likely to be "exploited" by commercial marketing aimed at manipulating consumer desires than by an online pervert or pornographer. Does our society want to have a conversation about these competing dangers and likelihoods?

A False Sense of Security

Still, in the end, filtering doesn't work primarily because it is easy for savvy students to get around it. Especially when young people are pooling resources and sharing what they find, there is no technological trick that will prevent them from finding something if they are determined to seek it out. . . .

Thinking we can keep young people from sites we don't want them to see simply by installing filters is whistling in the dark. If it works, it works only for the very young or the technologically naive. For the very young, it may be reasonable to protect them from inadvertent exposure to things they are not able to understand. But the older the child, the more pointless and self-defeating this effort becomes. The nature of the Internet is to expand access to information of all sorts—"good" and "bad." Because its basic ethos is one of openness, any attempts to filter, partition, or censor the Internet will be met aggressively by some skilled programmers and website developers, somewhere. For motivated young people, there will always be a way to get to what they are seeking. Ironically, filters could actually make the problem worse by lulling adults into a false sense of security, so that they supervise kids less (thinking that the filter is doing the job for them).

Periodical Bibliography

The following articles have been selected to supplement the diverse views presented in this chapter.

Melanie Asmar	"Filters Are Ineffective," *Concord Monitor/ Sunday Monitor*, February 6, 2006.
Michael Dobbs	"Experts Emphasize Interaction Over Security Measures," *Washington Post*, March 23, 2005.
Michael Dorn and Chris Dorn	"You Can Prevent Most School Shootings," *School Planning and Management*, November 2006.
Trent England and Steve Muscatello	"Six Years After Columbine? Time for Common Sense Again," Heritage Foundation, April 20, 2005. www.heritage.org.
Alorie Gilbert and Stefanie Olsen	"Do Web Filters Protect Your Child?" CNET News.com, January 24, 2006.
Larry A. Hicks	"Longtime Need for Detectors," *York Dispatch*, January 12, 2007.
Errol Lewis	"City's Kids Are Right to Fight," *New York Daily News*, November 17, 2006.
Pedro A. Noguera	"Re-Thinking School Safety," *In Motion*, June 2, 2004.
Jesse Nunes	"Virginia Tech Shootings Spark Questions, Debate," *Christian Science Monitor*, April 17, 2007. www.csmonitor.com.
NYSUT	"School Security," March 11, 2007. www.nysut.org.
Public Agenda	"School Safety," 2005.
Will Richardson	"To Block, or Not to Block," *District Administration*, February 2007.
Stan Simpson	"Detectors Don't Belong in Schools," *Hartford Courant*, September 27, 2006.

CHAPTER 3

Do School Policies
Respect Students' Rights?

Chapter Preface

In 2002, Joseph Frederick received from his high school principal a lengthy suspension for displaying a fourteen-foot banner that said, "Bong Hits 4 Jesus." His references to marijuana use and to Christianity were seen as controversial and potentially disruptive. However, he was not at school when he wielded the sign. He was across the street from his school at the Olympic Torch Relay, a public event. Administrators, arguing that the event was school-sanctioned, disciplined him for breaking the school's rule against promoting illegal substances. With the backing of the American Civil Liberties Union and other organizations, Frederick challenged his punishment in court based on his constitutional right to free speech. At the core of the issue is whether school codes banning offensive, disruptive, or harassing speech violate students' rights to free expression. Frederick's case was ultimately heard by the Supreme Court, and in June 2007 the Court ruled against the former student.

Critics blast school speech codes on the grounds that young people have a right to expression just as adults do. While most people concede that speech that is threatening or significantly disruptive should be limited at school, these critics charge that young people are too often punished for expressing themselves in harmless ways. In 2006, the Foundation for Individual Rights in Education found that 96 percent of the colleges studied banned expression that is constitutionally protected. A problem with rules governing speech at school, some assert, is that the vagueness of such rules allows school officials to go too far in punishing minor statements. University of North Carolina at Greensboro, for instance, prohibits "disrespect for persons," a policy that many people say is overbroad. As a result of speech codes, declares Eli Lehrer of *American Enterprise*, "Free speech no longer exists on American college campuses." Prohibiting speech that does not cause harm also teaches American youths that their rights do not matter, making them more likely to relinquish those rights when they become adults, free speech advocates contend. In any case, they argue, schools are educational institutions and therefore must allow open inquiry and reasoned argument even if it may offend some people. Lehrer points out, "No American court has ever upheld a right never to be offended."

Proponents of speech codes counter that schools are places of learning and have a special responsibility to make all students comfortable and safe. In fact, the case, *King v. M.S.D. of Washington Township* (2003) found that schools could be held liable for neglecting to protect students who are verbally threatened and later assaulted. Administrators and parents argue that students' freedom of expression should be limited if it may pose a threat to others or to the educational values of the school. David L. Stader, an associate professor at the University of Wyoming, is one member of this camp. He notes,

> Courts have never granted the same rights of expression to students on school grounds that ordinary citizens possess in everyday life. . . . Case law illustrates that students can be disciplined for verbal, written, or symbolic expression that is obscene, intimidating, or threatening.

In *Bethel School District No. 403 v. Fraser* (1986), for instance, the Court established that schools may deem certain speech inappropriate and subject to sanctions. Other cases demonstrate that disruptive, vulgar, and indecent expression may be prohibited whether it is expressed in school, off campus, or online.

The contentiousness of speech codes illustrates the difficulty of balancing the rights of students against the needs of administrators to maintain a safe and orderly learning environment. The authors in the following chapter struggle with this delicate balance.

| "Our biggest problem with a school uniform policy is the anti-individuality message it sends."

School Uniforms Stifle Freedom of Expression

Part I: Northwest Florida Daily News; Part II: Kent J. Fetzer

The authors of this two-part viewpoint contend that school uniform policies erode students' rights of expression. In part I, an editorial in the Northwest Florida Daily News *counters claims that uniforms ensure better behavior. Instead, it proposes, they suppress the individuality that administrators find distracting. In part II, Kent J. Fetzer of Salt Lake City, Utah, argues in the* Salt Lake Tribune *that abrogating students' rights of expression by mandating uniforms runs counter to the spirit and laws of our nation. Young people, he posits, should be allowed to choose clothing that is different from the norm as long as it meets standards of decency and poses no safety threat.*

As you read, consider the following questions:

1. How does the *Northwest Florida Daily News* editorial refute the argument that school uniforms ensure better behavior?

2. What advice does the editorial in the *Northwest Florida Daily News* offer to students who must wear uniforms?

3. According to Fetzer, what has long been a hallmark of our democracy?

The Borg, "Star Trek's" biomechanized bad guys, might as well have been talking about [Florida's] Okaloosa County's march toward school uniforms when they intoned: "Resistance is futile."

Indeed, as the *Daily News* reported last Monday [April 2002], more and more public schools are requiring or encouraging students to wear clothing of standardized colors and styles—uniforms, basically—and there's been nary a peep of protest. The goal: to mute some of the individuality that school administrators find so distracting.

Trekkers, however, will remind us that the Borg believed the individual was nothing and the collective was everything. That's one reason they were bad guys.

We don't think Okaloosa's uniform boosters are bad guys. But we do think they're emphasizing values that may not be, well, rewarding in the long run.

We know that many parents favor a uniform policy because it could make school clothes easier and cheaper to buy. And many administrators think uniforms will ensure kids behave better.

Anti-Individuality

Don't be too sure about that last one. If matching duds guaranteed better-behaved people, no soldier would ever go AWOL [absent without leave] and no prisoner would ever get into a fight.

But our biggest problem with a school uniform policy is the anti-individuality message it sends. If young people are to understand that a cornerstone of our freedom is the primacy

A Middle School Student Argues Against School Uniforms

By forcing children to wear uniforms to school, authorities are depriving them of their right of free expression. How do kids in middle school, or any grade level for that matter, mainly express themselves? Through their clothes. Wearing clothes that express one's personality, mood or feelings, is one of the few legal things a person can and will do to show what's on the inside. If someone is really energetic, she may possibly wear a bright skirt with a rainbow colored striped shirt and neon stockings. Someone else, on the other hand, may feel really angry, and wear red and black. "Clothes express yourself, your inner self," said Sean Henderson, 13, a seventh grader at Jefferson Middle School. "You might like to wear loud flashy clothing. If all you wear is dull white and navy blue, what does that say?" It says nothing. Everyone looks the same.

Alison Levine, Law Day Essay Contest First Place, Connecticut Attorney General's Office. www.ct.gov.

of the individual—over government, over the collective, over any non-voluntary association—then sticking them all into look-alike clothes is a poor way to teach it.

In our view, a splendid way to teach the values of freedom and responsibility is to let youngsters experience freedom and, in the process, learn to act responsibly.

Instead, more uniforms are being ordered.

Here's our advice to area students:

Make your own friends, form your own opinions and shape your own beliefs, even if you're forced to look like everybody else.

Think your own thoughts.

And hope that they don't find a way to stop that, too.

Part II

While we were still basking in the warm glow of a successful Olympics, proud of our American heritage, a little bit of our freedom slipped away from us. A somewhat harried Utah Legislature has recently engaged in some well-intentioned railroading of our rights, and now our governor has signed their encroachment into law.

I refer to House Bill 5, sponsored by Rep. Karen W. Morgan, D-Cottonwood Heights, which disallows parents' ability to opt out of mandatory wearing of school uniforms by their children. Many parents are in favor of the uniforms, but not all. The stage has thus been set for the rights of the minority to be abrogated by the tyranny of the majority, and this with the sanction of our state government.

An Infringement on Students' Rights

It may seem a trivial matter to some, but then again, should any loss of our basic personal freedoms be considered trivial? I think not. Freedom of expression has long been a hallmark of our democracy, and any loss of its privilege is deserving of our careful attention and scrutiny. It is insufficient that some may be disturbed by others' choices to be different. If a choice meets with common standards of decency and poses no threat to the safety and weal of the community, then the bar has not been met. Whereas, to infringe upon the rights and independence of the individual by coercing uniformity is an affront to both the spirit and the letter of the law of this great nation.

I know lawmakers' concern was protecting our children against the deleterious influence of gangs; but as I would not want my children imposed upon by these pernicious elements, or even unduly influenced by the peer pressure of fashion and fad, so also I would guard them from the tyranny of bureaucracy.

Studies have been adduced demonstrating improved scholastic performance in conjunction with the wearing of school uniforms. I will not attempt to gainsay these results other than to state that even if true, it is still insufficient justification to warrant encroachment upon the rights of an individual. Should teachers also be forced to wear uniforms in an effort to improve their teaching? And why not the general citizenry of the state, to improve our overall efficiency? If possible, would some wish even to control hair, eye, and skin color? The thought may seem ludicrous, but then, Hitler's Third Reich was to boast the blond-haired, blue-eyed Aryan race.

A nation that does not guard against small encroachments on its liberties is not likely to retain them. To suffer small erosions of our personal freedoms is to demonstrate our not being deserving of them. Vigilance has ever been the price of liberty, and ever will be.

> *"Uniforms instill discipline, help students focus on their studies and eliminate pressure on parents to outfit their kids."*

School Uniforms Do Not Stifle Freedom of Expression

Mike Kelly

According to Mike Kelly in this viewpoint, objections to school uniform policies are unfounded and frivolous. He especially takes issue with lawsuits filed against school districts on the grounds that the students' rights to choose clothing is a First Amendment freedom. One such case, he explains, is that of Mike DePinto, a fifth grader who wore a button depicting the Hitler Youth, a paramilitary group of Adolf Hitler's Nazi Party, to protest his school's uniform policy. In Kelly's view, requiring schoolchildren to don uniforms is a reasonable way to improve learning skills, discipline, and focus. Kelly has been a columnist for The Record *of Bergen County, New Jersey, for eighteen years.*

As you read, consider the following questions:

1. According to the author, how does DePinto's story get "weirder"?

2. What are Kelly's two main objections to Laura DePinto's statement, released by her son's lawyers?

3. In the author's view, what will DePinto's lawyers argue at trial?

Mike De Pinto, an 11-year-old fifth-grader from Bayonne [New Jersey], has a problem.

Just what kind of problem? This week [December 2006], a federal judge in Newark will try to find an answer.

We cherish our judicial system. For many, especially people on the downside of life, courts are often a refuge of last resort after stodgy bureaucracies and cowardly, narrow legislators refuse to act.

But sometimes, we waste judges' time with frivolous lawsuits.

Mike DePinto is wasting time.

At issue in this boy's life is a policy, invoked last September [2006] by the Bayonne public school system, that required students to wear uniforms to school.

DePinto is not necessarily claiming the school uniforms are ugly, distasteful or even too costly. If anything, the uniforms of khaki pants and blue shirts with a school emblem are probably too bland.

Style Issue

DePinto's dilemma is that he simply wants to pick his own clothes. Or as he put it to a Bayonne newspaper last week: "I'm opposed to somebody telling me what to wear and forcing me to wear an emblem against my will."

Against his will? An emblem?

We're not talking about DePinto being forced to put on a political or religious symbol. The school district merely wants him to wear a pair of khakis and a shirt with a school emblem on it.

What will DePinto say if he earns a spot on a high school athletic team in a few years? Would he tell his coach he wants to design his own uniform?

Incredibly, this story gets weirder.

What got DePinto in trouble with school authorities—and prompted his federal lawsuit—was not his objection to wearing a Bayonne uniform as much as how he accessorized it. He added a button with a photograph of Hitler Youth members in their trademark Nazi uniforms. DePinto claims his button, which has a red circle and a slash across the Hitler Youth photo and the slogan "No School Uniforms," is his personal form of protest.

The school district told DePinto and another student who later joined the button protest to get rid of the button or get suspended. Images of the Hitler Youth "are considered objectionable and are offensive to many Bayonne citizens and do not constitute free speech," the school district said.

DePinto, with the help of his mother and two Hackensack attorneys, filed a federal lawsuit along with the other protesting student, claiming that his freedom of expression was "stifled" because he had to remove his button. DePinto's attorneys tried to bolster their argument by claiming the Hitler Youth photo is "historically accurate" and "not very different from pictures found in history books used by American schools to teach social studies."

What's the legal logic here—that if Bayonne students can gaze at pictures of creepy Nazi kids in a history book they ought to be able to design a creepy button to wear on their school uniforms?

DePinto's mother, Laura, added to the ridiculousness with her own statement, released by her son's lawyers: "That image showed no swastikas, no weapons, and [Adolf] Hitler himself wasn't depicted. The picture makes a profound statement about what can happen when we turn children into 'uniform' followers."

Uniforms Ensure Equality

Given limited resources and legal authority, many public schools are using dress codes and uniform policies as one attempt to structure environments to enhance learning and development and diminish dress-related problem behavior and crime related to gangs. . . .

When students constantly compare their dress to others, and it seems to be the norm for many, uniformity in dress is viewed by some to be a great equalizer among children. The literature suggests there are advantages to a level playing field for growing children. Uniforms are thought by some to have a positive impact on [what some experts call] the "caste system stigma" that already exists for many minority children who struggle for competent identities in an oppressive, commercialized society. The president of the Long Beach [California] Board of Education voiced the expectation that school uniforms can have a major impact:

Uniforms help to create unity amid diversity by easing ethnic and cultural tensions and encouraging values of tolerance and civility. Uniforms also bridge differences between students and families of widely disparate income levels. Students from modest economic backgrounds are often the target of exclusion or ridicule on account of their dress. Even from the earliest grades, children feel the pressure to conform to idealized standards of dress, which may be beyond their family's means. Uniforms eliminate this pressure and allow the attention of students to be directed to learning and growing.

Rebecca A. Lopez,
Journal of Negro Education,
Fall 2003.

Profound Statement?

Memo to mom: Bayonne's students are not going to turn into the Hitler Youth because they are wearing khakis and blue shirts. Your statement is silly. So is the idea of using the name of Hitler as a vehicle to promote free expression.

There is a lively argument among some educators today about whether uniforms can be a useful tool in improving children's learning skills. Parochial and private schools have long followed a formula that uniforms instill discipline, help students focus on their studies and eliminate pressure on parents to outfit their kids to look like such paragons of scholarship as [pop stars] Justin Timberlake and Paris Hilton.

Now, public schools, from Secaucus to Hackensack, Fort Lee and Paterson, are considering various policies that would require students to wear some form of a uniform. But critics counter that uniforms don't really improve academics or student behavior and instead infringe on students' First Amendment rights of free expression.

Mike DePinto thinks he has a First Amendment case. On Monday, his attorneys are scheduled to present their arguments to U.S. District Court Judge Joseph A. Greenaway in Newark.

If only the judge would tell DePinto to button up and get back to school. But the judge probably won't do that.

He will likely allow lawyers to say that DePinto suffers deep sartorial pain each school day as he opens his closet and faces the cruel reality that he can't choose his own clothes and instead is forced to wear khaki pants and a blue shirt emblazoned with his school emblem. And then, we will hear the legal coup de gras: how he has a constitutional right to invoke the name of Adolf Hitler—and Hitler's memory of racism, anti-Semitism and mass murder—as a way of demonstrating all the pain he feels about the clothes on his back.

In uniform, can we all shout: Give us all a break? Go back to school.

If only the judge would do that.

"*Students assume that during [school] hearings they are entitled to the same protection afforded traditional trials. . . . This assumption could not be further from the truth.*"

Students' Due Process Rights Are Limited

Claire R. La Roche

In this viewpoint, Claire R. La Roche, assistant professor of business law at Longwood University in Virginia, stresses that students facing school hearings have fewer rights than people in court trials. Due process, defined by La Roche as a guarantee of fair procedures when a government impedes on a person's rights, is flexible. While students retain some of their due process rights, she claims, in disciplinary hearings they relinquish their right to a timely hearing and assistance of counsel. In academic dismissals, La Roche adds, students have even fewer rights and may be legally denied a formal hearing.

As you read, consider the following questions:

1. On what rationale is the distinction between disciplinary and academic dismissals based, according to a case quoted by the author?

Claire R. La Roche, "Student Rights Associated with Disciplinary and Academic Hearings and Sanctions," *College Student Journal*, March 2005, pp. 149–55. Copyright © 2005 Project Innovation (Alabama). Reproduced by permission.

2. According to the *Dixon* decision discussed by La
   Roche, what must a due process notice contain?

3. What did the U.S. Supreme Court determine in the
   Horowitz case regarding student rights, in the
   author's interpretation?

An important legal issue with significant implications for
both school administrators and students is whether students have due process rights associated with disciplinary and academic hearings. There are several common misconceptions regarding what process is due in connection with honor and judicial board hearings. Students assume that during these hearings they are entitled to the same protection afforded traditional trials in state or federal court. This assumption could not be further from the truth.

Due process is guaranteed by the Fifth and Fourteenth Amendments to the U.S. Constitution and is required whenever "a person's good name, reputation, honor, or integrity is at stake because of what the government is doing to him . . ." (*Wisconsin v. Constantineau*, 1971). The Fifth Amendment applies to the federal government and the Fourteenth Amendment provides that no state shall "deprive any person of life, liberty or property without due process of law." In other words, when actions of a state or the federal government affect a protected liberty or property right, due process guarantees fair procedures that include adequate notice and a meaningful opportunity to be heard. At state supported schools, students are guaranteed due process of law in connection with disciplinary proceedings and to a lesser degree with academic suspensions and dismissals.

Disciplinary Versus Academic Dismissals

Although case law has consistently held that the pursuit of an education is a right afforded the protection of the due process clause, the United States Supreme Court has indicated that "due process is flexible and calls for such procedural protections as the particular situation demands" (*Morrissey v. Brewer*, 1972). In fact, "there is a clear dichotomy between a student's due process rights in disciplinary dismissals and in academic dismissals" (*Mahavongsanan v. Hall*, 1976). State and federal court decisions have held that school disciplinary hearings require more stringent due process procedures than academic dismissals, even though an adverse decision may have the same effect on a student. This distinction is based upon the following rationale: "Misconduct is a very different matter from failure to attain a standard of excellence in studies. . . . A public hearing may be regarded as helpful to the ascertainment of misconduct and useless or harmful in finding out the truth as to scholarship" (*Barnard v. Inhabitants of Shelburne*, 1913).

Due Process in Disciplinary Hearings

Due process requires notice and an opportunity to be heard. Greater procedural safeguards are required in a dismissal hearing for violating rules of conduct in contrast to suspensions or expulsions for failing to meet academic standards. *Dixon v. Alabama State Board of Education* (1961) is a landmark case that articulated the standards of due process associated with disciplinary dismissals. The plaintiffs in the *Dixon* case were expelled from Alabama State College for requesting to be served at a white lunch counter and for participating in several mass demonstrations. Expulsion came without notice or an opportunity to be heard. The Fifth Circuit Court of Appeals held that due process requires notice and an opportunity to be heard before students at a tax-supported college may be expelled for misconduct. The notice should contain a statement of specific charges and grounds that could justify expulsion. The nature of the hearing depends upon the circumstances of the particular case. With a charge of misconduct, due process requires "something more than an informal interview with an administrative authority at the college" (*Dixon v. Alabama State Board of Education*).

The opinion in the *Dixon* case provides guidance on the nature of the notice and hearing standards. Although the court in *Dixon v. Alabama State Board of Education* did not require a 'full-dress judicial hearing' to comply with the rudiments of due process, the court indicated that the student be given the following:

- Names of the witnesses against him.

- An oral or written report of the facts to which each witness testified.

- The opportunity to present a defense before the disciplinary board or a college administrative official.

- The opportunity to produce supporting oral testimony or written affidavits.

The University of Virginia Cases

Several interesting cases involve the University of Virginia because the University's Honor System calls for a single sanction (dismissal) for breach of the Honor Code. One such case is *Cobb v. Rector and Visitors of the University of Virginia* (2000), a disciplinary dismissal involving academic dishonesty. Cobb argued that a nine-month delay between the time the professor accused him of cheating and the honor trial denied him the right to a timely hearing. In addition, Cobb claimed that he was not given a student-advisor for seven months prior to the trial. The District Court noted that a nine-month delay is not *per se* unconstitutional. Furthermore, the court noted that while having a student advisor during the pre-trial stage is advisable, it is not required by the due process clause.

Tigrett v. Rector & Visitors of the University of Virginia (2002) involved a disciplinary hearing in which three students were charged with disorderly conduct. The accused students challenged the fairness of the proceedings based on the fact that they were not present at their original hearing before the 1998 University Judiciary Committee (UJC). The UJC found the students responsible for the charges and recommended that they be expelled. However, on mandatory review, Vice President [William] Harmon ordered a new hearing based on perceived procedural irregularities, including trial *in absentia*. On rehearing, all three students were suspended. [Harrison] Tigrett and [Bradley] Kintz sued various officials of the University of Virginia under 42 USC § 1983 for violating their due process rights. The Fourth Circuit Court of Appeals rejected the allegation that the University deprived the students of their Fourteenth Amendment due process rights because they were not expelled from school by the initial 1998 UJC Panel, but suspended as a result of the subsequent hearing where procedures were consonant with due process of law.

Even Fewer Rights in Academic Dismissals

Students have even more limited due process rights associated with academic dismissals. Analysis of case law indicates that federal courts have been reluctant to interfere with school decisions based on academic performance, thus giving schools a great deal of discretion in judgments pertaining to academic evaluation resulting in suspension and expulsion of students.

The plaintiff in *Board of Curators of the University of Missouri v. Horowitz* (1977) was dismissed from medical school during her final year and filed a cause of action against the school based on a denial of her due process rights. Although Horowitz was notified by letters and in person of certain deficiencies in her hygiene and clinical performance prior to entering her fourth year of medical school, she was never given an opportunity to rebut these allegations at a formal hearing. Instead, a committee composed of the dean and members of the faculty decided that it was advisable to drop Horowitz

Due Process Rights Asssociated with Academic Dismissal and Disciplinary Hearings

Due Process Right	Academic Dismissal	Disciplinary Hearing
1. Timely Disposition	Mandatory but flexible	Mandatory but flexible
2. Notice	Mandatory	Mandatory
3. Adherence to established procedures	Recommended	Recommended
4. Hearing	Formal hearing not required	Hearing is mandatory Hearing not required for apppeals Accused has the right to be present
5. Assistance of Student Advocate	Not required	Advisable but not required
6. Right to Presence of Counsel	Not required	Unless criminal charges are pending, there is no right to have an attorney present.
7. Substantive Due Process	Required	Required

TAKEN FROM: Claire R. LaRoche, "Student Rights Associated with Disciplinary and Academic Hearings and Sanctions," *College Student Journal*, March 2005.

from the school. Horowitz made a written appeal to the provost but the provost approved the action of the committee. Ultimately, the Supreme Court of the United States held that procedural due process did not require a formal hearing when the school dismisses a student for academic reasons.

What Process Is a Student Due?

[The following items] provide guidance in establishing whether a school's academic dismissal and disciplinary procedures comply with minimum standards of due process. . . .

Timely Disposition. Due process mandates that students be afforded a fair hearing at a meaningful time. Unduly delaying a hearing hinders a student's opportunity to present a meaningful defense. However, case law indicates that a nine-month delay is not considered to be *per se* excessive.

The Notice. In order to mount an effective defense, a student should be given the specific nature of the accusations prior to the hearing. The Fifth Circuit Court of Appeals in *Dixon* held that "We are confident that precedent as well as a most fundamental constitutional principle support our holding that due process requires notice and some opportunity for hearing before a student at a tax-supported college is expelled for misconduct." According to the *Dixon* opinion "The notice should contain a statement of the specific charges and grounds which, if proven, would justify expulsion. . . ." It is suggested that a school inform a student of the charge, text of the rules on which charges are based, names of adverse witnesses, and possible sanctions.

Adherence to Established Procedures. Fundamental fairness suggests that a tax-supported school be consistent and follow its own procedures in handling academic dismissals and disciplinary matters. "Significant departures from stated procedures of government and even from isolated assurances . . . if sufficiently unfair and prejudicial, constitute procedural due process violations" (*Jones v. Board of Governors of the University of North Carolina et al.*, 1983). In *Jacobs v. College of William and Mary* (1980) the court noted that a college's failure to follow its own procedures is sufficient to deny an employee of procedural due process and thus may substantiate a §1983 claim for relief.

Nature of the Hearing. Although a formal hearing is not required in the case of an academic dismissal, it is mandatory when dismissal from a tax-supported school is based on a disciplinary charge. In the *Dixon* case, the Supreme Court noted "an opportunity to hear both sides in considerable detail is best suited to protect the rights of all involved. This is not to imply that a full-dress judicial hearing, with the right to cross-examine witnesses, is required." This hearing must be more than an informal interview and the judges must be impartial. In addition, students must be given an opportunity to present a defense and to produce either oral testimony or written affidavits of defense witnesses. Thus, a student should have the opportunity to be present at a disciplinary hearing and schools should avoid disciplinary hearings in absentia (*Tigrett v. Rector & Visitors of the University of Virginia*).

Additional Due Process Rights

Assistance of Student Advocate. Most courts have denied students the assistance of counsel. Assistance of counsel is not required for disciplinary or academic dismissals. To ensure procedural due process, the right to a student advocate is recommended, particularly in disciplinary proceedings.

Presence of Counsel. Unless criminal charges are pending, there is no right to have an attorney present (*Gabrilowitz v. Newman*, 1978). Gabrilowitz was charged with attempted rape and successfully argued that without counsel, his participation in the school hearing would create an unacceptable risk. The *Gabrilowitz* court held that due to the gravity of the situation and the pending criminal charges, the denial of the right to consult an attorney during the disciplinary hearing would constitute a denial of due process of law.

Substantive Due Process. In addition to procedural safeguards, the Fourteenth Amendment provides protection against arbitrary decisions with its substantive due process guarantee. In the *Dixon* case the court noted that while the government had the power to expel the plaintiffs from school, that power "is not unlimited and cannot be arbitrarily exercised." To ensure fundamental fairness, decisions must be based on the facts and supported by the evidence. Moreover, punishment should be commensurate with the severity of the offense. Consequently, it is important for schools to establish guidelines and be consistent with sanctions.

In the final analysis, the courts have held that due process is not an inflexible standard.

> "This [expansion of] due process . . .
> may encourage misconduct by making
> it much more costly for school officials
> to impose discipline."

Students' Due Process Rights Are Overbroad

Peter H. Schuck

In this viewpoint, Peter H. Schuck argues that students are afforded too many rights when it comes to school discipline. Too often, students invoke their rights to due process and challenge punishments imposed on them, he claims. In his view, this results in costly litigation for schools and permits those who "act out" to remain in class. Moreover, he maintains, students who are or claim to be disabled enjoy legal protections that he says prevent them from being appropriately punished. All of these factors harm students who wish to learn, Schuck says. Schuck is a Yale law professor and contributing editor of American Lawyer.

As you read, consider the following questions:

1. What were three findings of the 2004 Public Agenda survey, according to Schuck?

Peter H. Schuck, "Banish the Bad Apples," *American Lawyer*, October 2006, pp. 73–75. Reproduced by permission of the author.

2. What procedural rights are often granted to students even though the decision in *Goss* does not mandate them, in the author's view?

3. According to the author, what proportion of principals are prevented from suspending special education students for more than ten days straight in a school year?

The law has created many social programs to improve the conditions and opportunities of low-income individuals who are disadvantaged by factors beyond their control. Under this social contract, we provide insurance against certain random misfortunes—medical care for the indigent sick, unemployment benefits for those who lose their jobs, food stamps for the hungry or malnourished. In some of these programs, however, the vast majority of beneficiaries who play by the rules—the good apples—can be harmed by a few bad apples who act irresponsibly, immorally, or illegally. Well-intentioned laws often contribute to this problem by making it harder than it should be for officials to protect the many good apples from the few bad ones.

In our new book, *Targeting in Social Programs: Avoiding Bad Bets and Removing Bad Apples* (Brookings Institution Press), Richard Zeckhauser and I consider many varieties of bad apples. A common example is the public school student—sometimes all it takes is one—who chronically disrupts class and prevents many others who desperately need a sound education from learning. Another is the public housing tenant or homeless shelter resident whose repeated misconduct debases the quality of life of neighbors with no other place to go. Bad apples do more than simply waste scarce program resources and prevent good apple recipients from fully benefiting. They also cause taxpayers to stigmatize the entire group of beneficiaries and thus the program more generally, eroding its public support.

How Due Process Impedes Discipline

Between 1968 and 1975, students gained the right to due-process protections for the most minor aspects of day-to-day school discipline. ... *Goss v. Lopez,* [for instance] held that students facing short suspensions must be provided with "rudimentary" due process—an ill-defined concept that included such features as a right of students to know the charges against them. Other features of due process—such as the right to a formal hearing, the right to legal counsel, and the right to call witnesses—were mandated for more serious disciplinary infractions. After *Goss v. Lopez,* however, even low-level punishments (e.g., in-school detention or lowering a grade) were subjected to student and parental challenges in court.

Richard Arum, National Review, *October 11, 2004.*

The Dilemma Posed by Bad Apples

The bad-apple problem poses a daunting challenge for the law. Defining a bad apple is hard, necessitating tough line-drawing decisions. Identifying and classifying particular individuals as bad apples (for the purposes of administering a social program) may entail judgmental or predictive errors. Because the factors leading to individuals' misconduct are often complex and may be beyond their control, the idea of labeling anyone, particularly a youngster, as a bad apple seems harsh, even repellent; it smacks of "blaming the victim." This last objection, however, misses the main point: Society's highest priority must be to improve good apples' opportunities, even while attempting to address the problems of bad ones. This may require removing the miscreants until they can be rehabilitated, which also raises difficult legal issues, some of constitutional dimension.

People who must live in the same barrel as bad apples—
and thus stand to lose more from their misconduct—tend to
condemn their deviance, disruption, and violence even more
strongly than affluent people do, according to survey data.
Good apples' success in resisting the temptations and lures to
which bad ones succumb entails struggle, self-discipline, and
sacrifice. Social programs should support and reward their
hard-won achievements, not undermine them. Yet the reverse
often occurs, as many well-intentioned laws make it harder
than it should be for officials to protect the many good apples
from the few bad ones.

Due Process Rights Are Too Extensive

Consider the public schools. Public opinion polls and surveys
of both teachers and students reveal widespread, intense concern about the harm that disruptive students inflict on their
peers. This is not surprising. Just as students can learn from
each other as well as from their teachers, so, too, can one
student's misconduct quickly cascade through the classroom,
thereby jeopardizing learning for all. In a May 2004 study
conducted by the nonprofit opinion group Public Agenda, a
third of the teachers surveyed said that student discipline
problems had caused them or their colleagues to consider
leaving the profession; many had actually done so. Twenty
percent of parents reported that discipline problems had
caused them to consider moving (or to actually move) their
child to another school. Nearly eight in ten teachers said that
their school had students who should be removed and sent to
alternative schools. The same percentage reported that students are quick to remind them that they have rights or that
their parents can sue. A majority said that discipline problems
resulted from school officials backing down in the face of parents wielding aggressive lawyers. The survey also found that
both parents and teachers favored restricting the availability of
discipline-related lawsuits.

A recent book-length study by New York University professor and education specialist Richard Arum places much of the blame on judicial decisions that broadly extend due process rights to students, as well as on related educational regulations and legislation that constrain the authorities and often prevent them from taking prompt and effective action to curb disruptive behavior. The current situation is largely dictated by the U.S. Supreme Court's 1975 decision in *Goss v. Lopez*, which involved Columbus [Ohio] high school and junior high students who were suspended for ten days for fighting in the lunchroom. The Court extended due process rights—namely, notice and an opportunity to be heard—even to students facing relatively minor discipline such as short-term suspensions. Presumably, students facing more serious discipline—longer suspension, expulsion, or transfer to alternative programs—had more extensive procedural rights.

Post-*Goss* decisions have held that the constitutionally required hearing for a short-term suspension is minimal; an education lawyer, commenting in the *Education Law Reporter*, insists that *Goss* would be satisfied by "a three-minute due process. . . . Tell the student the charge. Give the student the opportunity to tell his/her side of the story, listen, and make a decision." The *Goss* hearing need not include written notice, presuspension notification of parents, an opportunity for parents to tell their side of the story, time to prepare a presentation, a right to counsel, a right to offer or cross-examine witnesses, or a right to appeal the decision. Nonetheless, state law and local school board policies often provide students with these additional procedural rights. Some courts, state laws, and administrative policies have extended these rights even to in-school suspensions or isolation, and out-of-school suspensions shorter than the ten days involved in *Goss*. This "due process creep" may encourage misconduct by making it much more costly for school officials to impose discipline.

IDEA Is Problematic

The Individuals with Disabilities Education Act (IDEA), enacted the same year as *Goss* was decided, conferred further substantive and procedural rights on students with learning-related disabilities. The statute defines these disabilities very broadly, and recent amendments have expanded the rights of disabled students, notably in discipline cases. IDEA limits schools' ability to remove disabled students from the classroom, particularly when their misconduct stems from their disability. This is a noble goal, but the statute has had the unanticipated effect of impeding the removal of bad apples, thereby blighting the educations of vast numbers of good-apple students.

IDEA does not seriously restrict removals for short periods or for violations related to weapons, drugs, or serious bodily injury. But schools cannot remove a disabled student for more than ten consecutive days for behavior falling short of "serious misconduct" and arising from the student's disability. In such a situation, parents are entitled to a statutory hearing to vindicate the child's right to a "free and appropriate" education. In practice, suspensions are infrequent and expulsions exceedingly rare, despite the widespread incidence of disruptive behavior. Of the more than 46 million public school students (disabled and not) in the government's database for the 2000–01 year, 6.6 percent received suspensions; only 0.21 percent were expelled. Although the rate of incidence of serious misconduct—violent behavior, possession of drugs or weapons—was more than three times higher among students with disabilities than among nondisabled students (50 per 1,000 versus 15 per 1,000), disabled students are seldom suspended or expelled. Many local school districts have adopted their own protections for disabled students, often imposed by court-mandated consent decrees, and these restrict disciplinary actions even more. Almost two-thirds of principals reported that they operate under a local policy that prevents them from suspending special education students for more than ten cumulative days in a school year.

Students are increasingly likely (through their parents) to challenge their school-imposed punishments in the courts. This trend, facilitated by legal changes concerning school discipline that began in the 1990s, has greatly complicated the school discipline problem. Public protest about disruptive and violent students possessing and selling weapons and drugs in the public schools led many states and school districts to adopt zero-tolerance disciplinary policies, often in the form of administrative rules authorizing or requiring school officials to impose a specific punishment for certain types of infractions. At the same time, however, Congress enacted laws protecting the disabled against discrimination in public programs, and expanded the IDEA rights of disabled students to avoid discipline for disability-related misbehavior.

Bad Apples Free to Terrorize Classmates

According to another study by Arum and his associates, this collision between public policies—those that increase schools' disciplinary options, and those that increase students' rights—has led to an unprecedented upsurge in lawsuits over school discipline. In this litigation, the courts have tended to uphold the schools in zero-tolerance cases, but have favored the students in cases in which they invoked disability. (Not surprisingly, the more affluent parents were most likely to appeal these cases.) Complaints about this new legal regime have centered on the schools' inability to quickly remove multiple and/or violent offenders who therefore remained to terrorize their classmates.

What happens to misbehaving students who are removed from school? According to a 2003 GAO [Government Accountability Office] report on special-needs students, short-term placements (that is fewer than ten days) were primarily either in suspension rooms at the school or at home; those removed for more than ten days were primarily placed in alternative schools or at home. Under New York City law, all students released from alternative programs must be placed in mainstream schools within five days of applying, and no school can turn them away. Unfortunately, we know less about alternative arrangements for nondisabled students. Critics decry many of them as "holding pens" where children are mistreated and denied adequate instruction. Good data on these programs is hard to come by (we could not get it from the New York and New Haven [Connecticut] school systems), but several points seem clear: Alternative programs are costly, and they can greatly benefit the good apples who remain in regular classrooms.

"By acknowledging students' right to form GSA's, you are not only . . . avoiding potential legal liability, you are supporting diversity in your schools."

Students Have a Right to Form Gay/Straight Alliances

American Civil Liberties Union

This viewpoint is a letter from the American Civil Liberties Union (ACLU) to school officials urging them to respect students' rights to form gay/straight alliances (GSAs) in school. GSAs, as the ACLU puts it, are extracurricular clubs that aim to combat discrimination and harassment of gays. Barring such clubs from school grounds, the ACLU insists, discourages open inquiry and contravenes the Equal Access Act, which states that schools that permit any club to operate must allow all *clubs to operate. The ACLU goes on to refute arguments by administrators who would ban GSAs for fear that allowing them will promote homosexuality or cause disruption. The ACLU states that its mission is to protect Americans' constitutional rights.*

American Civil Liberties Union, Foundation Lesbian and Gay Rights, James D. Esseks, "Letter to School Officials Regarding Gay/Straight Alliances," June 11, 2003. Reproduced by permission.

As you read, consider the following questions:

1. Which court case, according to the ACLU, found that most GSAs focus not on sex, but on issues related to sexual orientation?

2. How does the Supreme Court distinguish curricular from non-curricular clubs, in the organization's view?

3. What conditions does the ACLU claim schools might unlawfully place on GSAs but not on other clubs?

Students in your school are interested in forming a student organization, often called a gay/straight alliance, to focus on combating anti-gay harassment and discrimination and on educating the school community about these issues. Federal law requires that you treat such organizations the same as any other non-curricular club at your schools. But allowing the club to meet is not just a legal duty; it makes sense from an educational and a safety perspective, too.

Equal Access

According to the federal Equal Access Act [EAA], if a public high school allows any student group whose purpose is not directly related to the school's curriculum to meet on school grounds during lunch or before or after school, then it can't deny other student groups the same access to the school because of the content of their proposed discussions. Schools may not pick and choose among clubs based on what they think students should or should not discuss. As a federal judge concluded in one Equal Access Act case:

> The Board Members may be uncomfortable about students discussing sexual orientation and how all students need to accept each other, whether gay or straight. . . . [But] Defendants cannot censor the students' speech to avoid discussions on campus that cause them discomfort or represent an

unpopular viewpoint. In order to comply with the Equal Access Act, Anthony Colin, Heather Zeitin, and the members of the Gay-Straight Alliance must be permitted access to the school campus in the same way that the District provides access to all clubs, including the Christian Club and the Red Cross/Key Club.

—*Colin v. Orange Unified Sch. Dist.* (2000).

The judge went on to emphasize that the gay/straight alliance provides an important forum for students who are concerned about sexual orientation. Recognizing the impact of discrimination on gay youth, the judge wrote: "This injunction is not just about student pursuit of ideas and tolerance for diverse viewpoints. As any concerned parent would understand, this case may involve the protection of life itself."

In ruling as he did, the judge recognized that anti-gay harassment and violence are widespread among teenagers, especially in schools. Some of the most common epithets that teens use today to disparage each other are "faggot," "dyke," and "queer." A disproportionate amount of physical violence against gay men, lesbians, bisexuals, and transgendered people of all ages is perpetrated by teenage boys. Gay/straight alliances help to combat verbal and physical harassment. They create a space where students can come together to share their experiences, to discuss anti-gay attitudes they may experience in school, or to debate different perspectives on gay-related issues. Students talking openly and honestly with other students is a uniquely effective way of making young people aware of the harms caused by discrimination and violence.

School officials should not silence these student-initiated debates and discussions, as long as they do not involve targeted harassment of an individual student or group of students. Silencing ideas in a non-curricular setting because some people don't like them is not only incompatible with the educational values of open inquiry and wide-ranging debate that are central to our free political system—it is against the law.

The Equal Access Act was signed into law in 1984 after being heavily promoted by religious groups who wanted to ensure that students could form Christian clubs in public schools. The authors of the law understood that if this right were extended to students who wanted to start religious clubs, then it must be extended to all students.

Common Ways Schools Try to Block GSAs

Refusing to approve a GSA on the basis of morality: The Equal Access Act specifically provides that a school cannot deny equal access to student activities because of the "religious, political, philosophical, or other content of the speech at such meetings." Since any moral objections the school may have to a Gay/Straight Alliance are based on the religious, political, or philosophical views of its members, such an objection isn't recognized by the Act. Simply put, the school cannot ban a GSA based on issues of morality if the GSA doesn't interfere with the orderly conduct of educational activities in the school.

Refusing to approve GSA because the school doesn't want to be viewed as "endorsing homosexuality": Simply allowing a GSA to meet at a school does not indicate that the school approves or endorses the subject matter of the meetings. Observing that "the proposition that schools do not endorse everything they fail to censor is not complicated," the Supreme Court [in *Mergens*] has held that secondary school students are mature enough to understand that a school does not endorse or support speech that it merely permits on a nondiscriminatory basis. Congress recognized the same point, stating that "Students below the college level are capable of distinguishing between State-initiated, school-sponsored, or teacher-led religious speech on one hand and student-initiated, student-led religious speech on the other," [as quoted in *Mergens*]. In short, this excuse is no answer to a lawsuit that students can bring under the Equal Access Act.

Refusing to approve a GSA because the discussion of sex is not appropriate for high school students: In *Colin v. Orange Unified School District*, one of the many federal court cases in which the Equal Access Act rights of GSA's have been upheld, the court recognized that the focus of most GSA's is not sex, but issues related to sexual orientation and how to combat unfair treatment and prejudice. The court also noted that assuming a GSA will discuss sex and other clubs will not unfairly singles out the GSA based on a stereotype. Finally, as indicated by the fact that even religious groups in school sometimes discuss sex-related topics and sex-education is taught in classes, there is no reason to believe that high school students can't discuss sex-related topics. An administrator's discomfort is not sufficient reason to ban a GSA if the GSA does not create a substantial disruption.

Claiming the Law Does Not Apply

Refusing to approve a GSA because you think the Equal Access Act doesn't apply to the GSA at your school: As noted above, the protections of the Equal Access Act are triggered if the school allows just one non-curricular student activity on campus. While the Act itself doesn't define the differences between curricular and non-curricular clubs, a Supreme Court case does. In *Board of Education of the Westside Community Schools v. Mergens* (1990), the court held that a non-curricular student group is any group that doesn't "directly relate" to courses offered by the school. Let's say your school teaches swimming. A swim team or club would then be considered curricular; a scuba diving club would be considered non-curricular, even though it involves swimming. Groups like a chess club, a stamp-collecting club, a community service club, or a GSA are usually considered non-curricular, because what they do is not taught in any class.

The line between curricular student activities and non-curricular activities can be blurry, and schools that get it

A Gay Student Speaks of Her Fight to Found a Gay/Straight Alliance in Her High School

Every day there was some kind of harassment going on at school. We would bring it to a teacher's attention and nothing would happen. . . .

I knew that starting the gay-straight alliance would cause controversy, yet I had no idea that the community would be in an immediate uproar. Everyone tried to justify themselves with the Bible to back up their hatred.

I became discouraged when I felt nothing was going my way. Then I thought of Martin Luther King Jr. and [Mohandas] Gandhi: If they had given up when things got rough, where would we be now? Everyone has the right to be who they are. I believe that it shouldn't be so hard to be yourself. . . .

No one has the right to silence anyone for any reason. We want to let all voices be heard, including those of LGBT [lesbian, gay, bisexual, and transgendered] students.

Kerry Pacer, quoted in Alan Sverdlik,
Advocate, June 21, 2005.

wrong can pay a high price. For example, a school district in Kentucky recently thought that the Equal Access Act did not apply to it because, in its view, the school had no non-curricular clubs on campus. A federal judge held otherwise, noting that the school's community service club, drama club, and class officer organizations continued to meet and were not "directly related" to the curriculum.

Even if a school successfully eliminates all non-curricular clubs, it may still have to allow a GSA to meet if that group is curricular. In Utah, a school district eliminated all non-curricular clubs in an attempt to prevent a GSA from meeting. The GSA students simply formed a different club, whose purpose was to discuss subjects taught in the school's curriculum such as American government and law, U.S. history, and sociology, but from a lesbian and gay rights perspective. When the school rejected the students' application, the students sued. The court held that the school was not applying its policy evenly because it was allowing a very broad interpretation of "curricular" for some groups but not others, and ordered the school to recognize the club.

In short, trying to prevent a GSA from meeting by eliminating all non-curricular clubs, or by limiting the kind of curricular clubs that can meet, is asking for a lawsuit. It also imposes a significant and unjustifiable cost on all students, depriving them of numerous after-school activities simply in order to silence students concerned about harassment and discrimination. That's just not a proper role for a school.

Applying Unfair Standards

Refusing to approve a GSA because a GSA will cause disruption: When there is disruption surrounding a GSA, school officials need to ask themselves, "Who's really being disruptive here?" If students, parents, or community members get in an uproar because they don't like a GSA, *they* are the ones causing the disruption—not the GSA itself. A court in Kentucky recently ruled that even extensive disruption in the community and in school (thousand-person rallies, a boycott by half the student body) isn't enough to justify shutting down a GSA where the GSA members themselves are not causing the commotion.

Refusing to approve a GSA, claiming that it is under the control of some outside group or organization: Although most high school clubs that address LGBT [lesbian, gay, bisexual, and transgender] issues are referred to as GSA's, and although some national organizations like the Gay, Lesbian, Straight Education Network have attempted to compile informal contact directories of GSA's across the U.S., GSA's remain local and student-driven. There is *no* national organization or governing body for GSA's.

A school must apply restrictions regarding involvement of non-school persons uniformly. For example, if other clubs have names from outside organizations (for example a Key Club) and have not been prohibited, then the school cannot deny the GSA approval based on its name.

Imposing conditions on the GSA that don't apply to other clubs: Schools cannot subject GSA's to any conditions that do not apply to all other non-curricular clubs. Requiring a faculty advisor for the GSA but not for other groups, or placing different requirements on a GSA's posters, leaflets, and announcements than it places on other groups, are examples of differential treatment that's unlawful. In addition, delaying acting on the GSA's application for approval can itself be disparate treatment that violates the EAA.

Requiring a GSA to change its name: Many clubs want to use the name Gay/Straight Alliance, although some come up with other names (one group wanted to call itself Helping Unite Gays and Straights, or "HUGS"). Whatever the name is, schools cannot require that any reference to sexual orientation be removed, since doing so changes the focus and goals of the club. The court in *Colin* specifically ruled that a school could not tell a GSA to remove the term "gay" from its name.

We hope this letter has given you a firm understanding of why schools should allow GSA's to form as well as how you can remain in compliance with the Equal Access Act. By acknowledging students' right to form GSA's, you are not only obeying the law and avoiding potential legal liability, you are supporting diversity in your schools and taking a strong step towards addressing anti-gay harassment.

| "If a school allows ['gay' clubs], it sets the precedent for other harmful clubs for students as well as the future unlimited demands of 'gay' activists."

Students Do Not Have a Right to Form Gay/Straight Alliances

Linda P. Harvey

Linda P. Harvey is president and founder of Mission: America, a nonprofit organization that educates Christians about cultural issues. In this viewpoint, she decries the efforts of gay advocates to establish gay/straight alliances in schools, clubs that she says promote homosexuality. Because homosexuality is physically and emotionally detrimental, in Harvey's opinion, youths should be discouraged from approving it. Gay/straight alliances should also be opposed, she claims, because they disrupt schools, facilitate homosexual abuse, and encourage sexual experimentation. Enforcing school harassment codes is a better way to prevent discrimination than setting up gay clubs, she reasons.

As you read, consider the following questions:

1. What was the original purpose of the Equal Access Act, in Harvey's view?

Linda P. Harvey, "No 'Equal Access' for Homosexual Clubs: How to Keep GSA's Out of Your Child's School," Mission: America, 2003. Reproduced by permission.

2. According to the author, the objective of gay/
straight alliances to reduce homophobia is shorthand for what?

3. What does Harvey claim are eight topics of discussion in gay clubs?

It starts with a handful of students. They want a club in
their high school—or sometimes nowadays it's a middle
school. They want to meet with others who have their same
interests and concerns. They say they have a right to meet
based on the federal Equal Access Act, which provided opportunities for school Bible groups to meet in high schools as
non-curricular clubs. These students say there shouldn't be
discrimination against their particular type of club, either.

But what responsible school would permit students to organize a tattoo club?

High-Risk Behavior Is Being Encouraged

Surely no responsible school would allow such a dangerous,
risky behavior to be legitimized by a school club. Yet, according to the Gay, Lesbian and Straight Education Network
(GLSEN), as of the end of 2002, almost 1,700 homosexual
clubs now exist in schools in the U.S. So why not a tattoo
club? Or a Marlboro club? Or a pornography club? Or a diet
pills club? Or a drag racing club? Or a nudists' club? All are
unacceptable activities, and we are unaware of any such organizations in U.S. high schools. Yet clubs centered around a
known high-risk behavior like homosexuality are allowed,
sometimes even encouraged. Schools seem willing to believe
the unsubstantiated claims of homosexual activists and their
student allies that these clubs are a fair civil rights' gesture to
a pre-existing minority, and that students will simply share
philosophical views at their meetings. No high-risk sexual behavior will be discussed, organizers assert. Yet drag racing, potentially fatal diet schemes and other topics could similarly

only be approached "ideologically"—yet parents in most communities would have a fit.

In the current youth culture, it's becoming more acceptable to be homosexual or bisexual. These identities and the behaviors associated are "in" and "cool" in many schools, after a decade of relentless promotion. However, clubs encouraging more acceptance of this behavior are completely inappropriate.

But homosexual clubs are needed, legal activists like the ACLU [American Civil Liberties Union] and Lambda Legal Defense Fund assert, because students with homosexual desires are victims of discrimination, harassment that goes unpunished, and suffer from a higher risk of suicide. Questionable statistics, seldom challenged, accompany these claims. In those schools where bullying has been a problem, however, is the solution to force everyone to accept homosexuality? Why not simply document with facts any real problems, then enforce existing conduct codes for everyone?

The "Equal Access" argument has once again moved to center stage since the ACLU filed suit in January [2003] to force a "gay" club at a school in Ashland, KY, and in March, at a school in Klein, TX. Now, many schools are giving in to student activist demands on this issue. School officials in Klein have quickly caved in to ACLU pressure and allowed the club to go forward, despite the fact that sodomy is still illegal in that state.

Many believe there are ways to prevent impressionable students from this kind of harmful application of the Equal Access Act, but to do so will call upon the courage, good sense, and proactive planning of communities and schools.

The Distortion of Equal Access

How did this 1984 federal law come to be misused to allow sodomy and cross-dressing to become implicitly acceptable behaviors in so many U.S. schools?

The Equal Access Act was passed because many schools were barring school Bible or Christian clubs citing "separation of church and state" as a justification. This phrase appears nowhere in our Constitution but reflects judicial opinion based on a letter written by Thomas Jefferson to a Baptist group, assuring them there would be no official state religion. So in 1984, Congress had to pass an unnecessary law to re-assert what our Constitution allowed for all along—that a group of students should be able to organize a religious club based on their First Amendment rights and have it recognized within their school.

Now this law has been used in the last decade as justification for "gay" clubs to organize. Courts have said that "equal access" applies if the school has other non-curricular clubs because of First Amendment rights, i.e., freedom of speech. A curricular club would be like, e.g., a French Club. A non-curricular club would be something like the Chess Club or Future Business Leaders of America Club. The club must be open to all students and truly be student-organized with no adults or outside organizations backing the club. All of these provisions only apply to schools which accept federal funds in some way.

Yet schools still have the authority, courts have determined, to exclude clubs that would cause significant disruption or would interfere with order. The school can still act to "protect the well-being of students and faculty," [according to Lambda Legal Defense Fund]. One would think this would be a sound reason to exclude any club advocating homosexuality. Amazingly, very few schools are taking this stand. Why?

Many times, administrators and school boards support the clubs after being convinced this constitutes "tolerance." They are also bombarded with pro-homosexual information supporting such equal access by the NEA [National Education Association] and other sympathetic groups. They erroneously believe that homosexuality is an inborn trait that some students simply will at some point discover is a part of their make-up. There are schools that would prevent the formation of these clubs if they could, but when threatened by well-funded, mighty legal defense groups like the ACLU or Lambda Legal Defense Fund, they scramble to put together a strategy. Having failed to prepare adequately, they give up and give in.

Steps to Prevent "Gay" Clubs

We believe that schools can defend against this assault on high standards and healthy behavior. There are many reasons that are in the best interests of all students and the community to oppose "gay" clubs. If a school allows this, it sets the precedent for other harmful clubs for students as well as the future un-limited demands of "gay" activists. This greatly endangers the students who want the club as well as others.

Based on the provisions already allowed for under "Equal Access" and with additional thorough research, schools may be able to successfully defend themselves against homosexual clubs and all that follows. Here are some suggested steps:

Health and Legal Risks

Take an official school position, with supporting research, that homosexuality, bisexuality and gender confusion are threats to student physical and mental well-being. In today's climate, this takes a lot of guts, but it is a winnable position, because not only is it the truth, it's the opinion of most parents. A recent Zogby poll clearly showed that, when given the facts, parents overwhelmingly object to having their kids taught to accept homosexuality as equal to heterosexuality.

Health information will provide ample evidence of the po-tential for harm. It should include information on the high risk of AIDS in this country by males having sex with males (MSM) as well as the much-higher risk of other STDs [sexu-ally transmitted diseases] by practicing homosexuals. The higher rates of promiscuity, domestic violence and much-lower life span should be covered as well as the lack of any evidence for a gay "gene."

One critical part of any school district's defense should be to provide evidence, by researching "gay" advocacy material, of the overwhelming promotion to youth of just the opposite of a fixed, stable sexual identity. The real goal is for all people, including youth, to be able to practice sexual fluidity and experimentation (which would include homosexual behavior), even by those who call themselves "heterosexuals." There is no question that this broad strategy of fluid sexualization of youth is having an impact and adversely affecting our kids. This bottom line of the "gay" agenda is its soft underbelly that, when exposed and fully explained, will alarm parents as they should be, and discourage support for pro-homosexual activities in schools. . . .

Another solid argument, as an extension of the health risks, is the issue of school liability. What will be the future pay-outs for the district when the fifteen-year-old who is seduced into homosexual behavior through attendance at "gay" club meetings contracts AIDS, and in six years when he is 21, sues your district?

The fact is that homosexual desire can change. Many times, it is the troubled youth who is drawn to these attractions and behavior. Sometimes the influence of older teens, or a homosexual teacher or coach, is a factor, and these will be the people involved in your school's "gay-straight alliance," the name often given to these clubs. Responsible counseling should be advising youth to turn away from homosexual desire and avoid these deadly consequences. There will be no defense before a jury of Mom and Pop Americans who cannot believe that your school supported a "gay" club, implying that the behavior was innocuous and acceptable. And always-greedy liability lawyers will be seeking out such cases just like medical malpractice, once one proves successful.

Corruption of Minors

Then there is the molestation issue. Openly homosexual adults will come into contact with your "gay" club members, especially after it gets rolling and is well-established. They may be invited as guest speakers, or a homosexual may be a teacher advisor. Homosexuals are much more inclined to seduce young teens than heterosexuals, in part because close access is allowed to same sex youth in a way not available between adults and youth of the opposite sex. Corruption of a minor is still illegal everywhere in the U.S.

Also, as can be easily verified, homosexual teens are told by advocates that sex between adults and minors is part of their "empowerment" to make their own sexual decisions early. As Mission America has documented, this activity is a frequent refrain of pro-homosexual groups and material, which your "gay" club members will use as their resources and guidelines. The 30-year-old "Pride Day" speaker with undisclosed HIV infection who meets and then seduces the 15-year-old president of your "gay" club after a school-sponsored event will provide disastrous great headlines for your school. Think of the current predicament of the Catholic Church, and act accordingly to protect your district's financial status and your students. . . .

A school club will imply that homosexual behavior is acceptable and non-threatening, and if a school district wants to maintain otherwise, then why NOT a smoking club, or a Ku Klux Klan club? The reason is, of course, to avoid any implication of school endorsement of certain behaviors or philosophies, as well as for liability reasons. The same argument should apply to homosexual clubs. If your school has a non-discrimination code citing "sexual orientation," it will be harder to fight a homosexual club. A very valuable step would be to revoke that code, but if it must remain, it can be argued that this code was only meant to increase politeness and civil-

Student Indoctrination into Homosexual Views

To raise an entire new generation of young people who will have an unquestioning acceptance of pro-homosexual dogma requires activities that will reach the entire student body.

These usually begin with special assemblies or one-day or one-time events. For example, when a school in Massachusetts celebrated "To B GLAD Day," parents were not told that it stood for "Transgender, Bisexual, Gay and Lesbian Day," and would feature workshops about "Life Outside the Gender Norm," "Being Gay in the Professional World," and "fighting homophobia." . . .

Pro-homosexual activists also try to fill school libraries and required reading lists with books that not only present homosexuals in a positive light, but describe homosexual acts being committed by young people in explicit terms.

One such book, assigned to a high school class in Massachusetts, is written from the perspective of a teenager, who describes (according to the Associated Press) "his friend's first homosexual experience, a kid who got so drunk that he had sex with a dog, and a girl and boy who have sex on a golf course."

Peter Sprigg, "Steering Them Wrong:
How Schools Push Kids to Accept Pro-Gay Dogma,"
Family Research Council, www.frc.org.

ity, not to endorse these behaviors. You need to establish your own definition of the squishy term "discrimination" before they do.

A Threat to Traditional Values

Reaffirm the known, clear risks of homosexuality as opposed to abstinence by students, which should be the standard. If abstinence until marriage is not the standard in your school, it should be. There are many benefits and no detriments to delaying sexual activity until marriage. This can be remedied by passing a district policy along these lines.

Show how this club will disrupt order and civility. The club's objective is to discuss the need to reduce harassment and "homophobia," which they will, if pressed, reveal is their shorthand for what is usually open hostility toward traditional values, parental and school authority, and the views of many traditional religions. This will create divisiveness in the school in new, and not constructive, ways. It will increase intolerance, bias and stereotypes, because homosexual activist students are being taught by all the major advocacy organizations to fear and fight parents who try to restrict their sexual freedom; schools that don't jump to their every demand; and religions like traditional Christianity, conservative Judaism, conservative Hindu faith and conservative Islam.

Their harassment claims can be dealt with simply by ensuring that the current school conduct code is being enforced fairly, but after that, don't give in to the endless demands for "non-harassment" policies based on sexual orientation. Any student who is assaulted or whose property is vandalized needs to be protected, and the harassers punished but not based on pre-set objectionable thought. It should be based on the severity of the incident. Insults will need to be dealt with on a case by case basis, and falls into a subjective realm. Don't paint the district into the unnecessary corner of endorsing homosexuality simply to protect some students from excessive insults. Punish all those who are excessive verbal harassers, whatever the content.

An Endorsement of Homosexuality

Demonstrate that a homosexual club does, in fact, communicate endorsement to students of homosexual behavior by any student who wishes to engage in it. It is not simply, as will be claimed, justice for a small, fixed minority group. The club will be open to anyone. There will usually be a demand that the club to be open to students without parental knowledge. They will discuss homosexuality, bisexuality, and cross-gender identity, dress and the benefits of sex change surgery and/or hormones. They will talk about homosexual liaisons, provide information about web sites that contain graphic homosexual pornography, community social outlets where homosexual activity will be facilitated, and provide opportunities for students to participate. This is a critical point and key to your public relations and media communications on this issue. A "gay" club is not for a pre-existing minority, even though only a small group at present will be interested in it, and this is how it will be portrayed by its organizers (and they probably truly believe this). No such minority exists, but those students wishing to engage in homosexual activity or cross-dressing are a flexible and changeable sub-section of the whole student body.

More students are likely to be drawn into homosexual activity as a result of the existence of this club. This usually manifests as an increase in expressed "bisexuality" by more students. Homosexual-friendly books tell students this is okay. The books endorsed by GLSEN [Gay, Lesbian and Straight Education Network] and PFLAG [Parents, Families and Friends of Lesbians and Gays] which we've researched reveal that sexual fluidity and experimentation by any student who wishes to engage in it is the goal—not "rights" for only a few. ALL district parents therefore will need to be notified in these terms. Make this a condition if your school is forced into accepting a "gay" club—that all the district's parents will need to be advised and that you must do this for liability reasons.

Student activist members of "gay" clubs and their adult allies will insist your school support radical pro-homosexual district-wide activities. Once your school allows a "gay" club, student activists will demand—or else go to the media and complain—that your school hold Pride Days, Transgender Awareness Days, "Coming Out" days, etc. Your school can also expect to have teachers who are openly homosexual apply for positions, or "come out" if they already hold them. If the school objects, you will be sued, and they will win based on "discrimination." Then you may have teachers or students who are cross-dressers or have had a sex change do the same thing. This again opens up a whole new range of possible dangers for students and liability risks for the district.

Periodical Bibliography

The following articles have been selected to supplement the diverse views presented in this chapter.

Richard Arum   "Sparing Rods, Spoiling Children: The Impossibility of School Discipline," *National Review*, October 11, 2004.

Associated Press   "Buttars Seeks Support from Eagle Forum," January 15, 2006. www.heraldextra.com.

John Caldwell   "Gay Straight Revolution," *Advocate*, June 21, 2005.

Timothy J. Dailey, Don Schmierer, and Peter Sprigg   "Homosexuality and Children: The Impact for Future Generations," Family Research Council. www.frc.org.

Edwin C. Darden   "Search and Seizure, Due Process, and Public Schools," Center for Public Education, April 5, 2006.

Jessica DuLong   "Are Schools Invading Your Privacy?" *Cosmo-Girl!*, April 2005.

Charles C. Haynes   "T-Shirt Rebellion in the Land of the Free," First Amendment Center, March 14, 2004.

Spokesman-Review "School Board Adopted Reasonable Club Policy," June 26, 2006.

Yuma (AZ) Sun   "Rights of Child Limited and Not Same as Adult," July 2, 2006.

Kaitlyn Whiteside   "School Dress Codes Get a Bad Rap, But They Make Life, Expressing Yourself Much Easier." *Chattanooga Times/Free Press*, November 20, 2006.

Michael Paul Williams   "School-Clubs Bills Appeal to Homophobia," *Richmond Times-Dispatch*, January 22, 2007.

What School Policies Are Needed in the Future?

Chapter Preface

In recent years, at least forty-three American college campuses and many high schools have implemented smoking bans. While most schools prohibit tobacco use indoors and the use by minors, many new policies also bar smoking outside, near building entrances and in stadiums, even for adults. More restrictive bans outlaw smoking anywhere on school grounds, including open spaces and students' dorm rooms.

Supporters of these bans cite research on the dangers tobacco poses not only to smokers but to anyone nearby who inhales the smoke. A report by former U.S. Surgeon General Richard H. Carmona claims that secondhand smoke contains higher concentrations of toxins than a smoker inhales and can raise a nonsmoker's heart disease and lung cancer risks by 20 to 30 percent. At a press conference, Carmona explained: "Brief exposure can have immediate harmful effects on blood and blood vessels, potentially increasing the risk of a heart attack. Secondhand smoke exposure can quickly irritate the lungs, or trigger an asthma attack." The consequences, he cautioned, can be deadly.

With these factors in mind, Blake Bivens, a volunteer of the American Cancer Society, lambasted two senators for voting down a smoking ban in Tennessee schools. He writes, "Our young people deserve more than hollow words—they deserve substantive action to protect their health." Many students, it seems, support tobacco bans, with 63 percent of students at Santa Monica College in California, for instance, voting to make the campus smoke-free. Since her college restricted smoking, sophomore Rachel Klein observes: "I feel better. I'm not breathing in smoke all the time." Discussing a ban has made another student, Lisa Chaffin, especially aware of her addiction. She imagines herself fleeing campus in the middle of class because she needs a cigarette so badly. "These thoughts are kind of a wake-up call," she admits. "Maybe now that I can't smoke on campus, it will be the extra motivation I need to quit." Moreover, some people assert, adults should be barred from smoking at school because it sets a bad example for youths. Studies indicate that schools where greater numbers of older students smoke have higher smoking initiation rates among younger students.

Those on the other side of the debate counter that adults should be permitted to engage in a legal activity at the place where they spend the better part of their day. Matthew Madden of Santa Monica College discusses what he sees as hypocrisy: "We can die on the front lines of war for our country, we can vote, we can buy the cigarettes, and slowly but surely, yet another place we can't smoke them." Other smokers dread coming to class if they cannot enjoy a cigarette anywhere on campus. It makes school even more difficult, they complain. They especially take issue with school-wide bans that do not allow outside smoking areas. "I don't see anything wrong with smoking outside," comments Ryan Estomo of Cosumnes River College in Sacramento. "They should have at least one designated area out in the open for smokers to go to." Furthermore, some claim, it is unnecessary to restrict smoking in student housing because smokers are already segregated from nonsmokers in dorms. In most smokers' view, it is also impractical to go outside for a cigarette in bad weather.

Whether schools should enact restrictive smoking policies is just one of several debates administrators are currently engaged in. As the arguments in chapter 4 indicate, new developments such as cell phones and cyberbullying fuel the controversy over what technologies and behaviors schools need to regulate in the future.

| "Students survived for hundreds of years without cell phones and they don't need them now."

Cell Phones Should Be Banned in Schools

Armstrong Williams

In this viewpoint, Armstrong Williams recommends prohibiting cell phones in school because, in his opinion, they are distracting to the user and to other students. Cell phones, he claims, are used to send text messages during class, browse sexual content on the Internet, cheat on tests, and even coordinate drug deals on school grounds. Regulating the use of cell phones in schools puts undue stress on administrators and teachers, he explains. A Christian conservative, Williams writes nationally syndicated columns and hosts radio and television shows.

As you read, consider the following questions:

1. In what two ways did Councilwoman Letitia James respond to the cell phone ban, in the author's assertion?

2. The notion that cell phones should be allowed in schools for safety is comparable to what other idea, according to Williams?

Armstrong Williams, "Classrooms Are No Place for Cell Phones," Townhall.com, June 26, 2006. Reproduced by permission of the author. www.armstrongwilliams.com.

3. In the author's view, how do students use cell
phones to incite violence?

L ast month [May 2006] Mayor [Michael] Bloomberg and
Schools Chancellor Joel Klein teamed up to ban cell
phones from New York public schools. As expected, uproar
ensued, but you may be shocked at where the racket came
from. No, it was not the students who were up in arms about
having their precious lifelines taken away. It was the local po-
liticos and parent groups who most opposed the ban.

An Uproar by Parents and Politicians

When I first heard about the cell phone ban for New York
schools, I figured students would most vehemently oppose the
ban. I guessed that they would be so disappointed about losing the opportunity to text-message their friends while in
class, take pictures during breaks, surf the internet during lec-
tures, and talk on the phone between periods that they would
do all they could to overturn the ban. Instead, these students
simply adjusted to the new rules and went back to the good
old days of passing notes under the desks. But their parents
and politicians did not back down so easily.

Public Advocate Betsy Gotbaum, city Controller William
Thompson, several ranking members of the City Council, including Education Committee Chairman Robert Jackson and
Land Use Committee Chairwoman Melinda Katz, all came out
against the ban. A parents' group collected more than 1,200
signatures on a petition opposing the ban. And City Councilwoman Letitia James (Brooklyn) introduced legislation calling
for a moratorium on cell phone confiscation. James also is exploring whether the Council has the authority to override
Mayor Bloomberg and Klein on the issue, she said.

Excuses

Parent and political groups claim that students need the
phones before and after school for safety and security reasons.

A Court Decision Upholds a School District's Ban on Cell Phones

After considering the arguments of the parties, this Court concludes that the questioned aspect of the Cell Phone Rules, i.e., the ban on possession of cell phones in schools, without prior authorization (as distinct from a ban on cell phone use), has a rational basis. Accordingly, this Court may not set them aside as Petitioners have sought under the court's powers.

Any enforcement system focusing on use, rather than possession, requires teachers, rather than only security personnel at the school door, to observe and enforce the ban and become involved in confronting students and punishment decisions, in detriment of their pedagogical mission, both by reducing their time teaching and by increasing their perception as an adversary to students. Further, it is not inappropriate to conclude that a use ban may be more disruptive than a possession ban. Under a use ban, cell phones will be carried by teenagers and tweens (and maybe even younger children) whose self control may not be perfectly formed. DOE [Department of Education] therefore had a rational basis to project that a possession ban would lead to less distraction and disturbance to the educational mission of the school.

Lewis Bart Stone,
Camella Price et al. v. New York Board of Education et al.,
Supreme Court of the State of New York, May 7, 2007.

They cite the scarce supply of pay phones and the non-existent after school programs as reasons why cell phones are needed to arrange for transportation or deal with an emergency. Also, most parents enjoy the idea of being able to contact their child at a moment's notice to inquire about their whereabouts and current activity.

I am shocked and disappointed that some parents and politicians believe that cell phones as safety devices are a worthy tradeoff for disruptions at school. That philosophy is comparable to claiming that weapons should be allowed in school to prevent after school attacks. Frankly, it just doesn't make sense. Students survived for hundreds of years without cell phones and they don't need them now. If parents are seriously worried about the safety of their children, they can take other steps to ensure their safety. A cell phone is not the answer.

Support Teachers by Upholding the Cell Phone Ban

Public schools have become war zones with teachers and administrators acting as the unequipped arbitrators. Cell phones are a big reason these behavior problems are occurring in schools everywhere around the country. Students are inciting violence by calling gangs and older kids anytime an argument occurs, running away from teachers who see them talking on the phone, and turning their cell phone ring tones to a pitch that adults cannot notice because of hearing deficiencies. Students are downloading inappropriate movies and images and sharing them between friends which disrupts class and can lead to sexual harassment situations. Students are using cell phones to cheat by either taking pictures of their answer sheet, sending the image to other fellow students or even by text-messaging the answers. They also use cell phones to coordinate drug deals and to call into schools where they fake absences by pretending to be their parents or other false identities. Besides distracting the cell phone users, other students are unable to focus because of cell phone disruptions.

Cell phones put unneeded stress on teachers and administrators as they exhaust all of their tools to reach students. Kids today are more rebellious, more disrespectful and more undisciplined than ever. Adults need to take a stand and give kids more boundaries, not more freedom. This discipline starts at home, but it spreads to school as well. If teachers agree with the Mayor's ban (which they overwhelmingly do), then parents and politicians should too. Teachers have a tough enough job as it is and we must make it easier for them by upholding this ban on cell phones at schools.

> *"Why hurt the thousands of parents and students who use the cell phones appropriately—only to and from school or in cases of emergency?"*

Cell Phones Should Not Be Banned in Schools

Randi Weingarten

Randi Weingarten, president of United Federation of Teachers (UFT), submitted an affidavit on behalf of her organization in a 2006 court case challenging a cell phone ban in New York City schools. This viewpoint is excerpted from that affidavit. While Weingarten concedes that cell phone use in schools can be disruptive, she asserts that a widespread ban is unnecessary. Instead, she suggests, each school should develop its own policy, which may require that cell phones be turned off in class but should allow their use before and after school and in case of emergency.

As you read, consider the following questions:

1. How does Weingarten explain educators' unique role and responsibilities in the instruction of schoolchildren?

Randi Weingarten, affidavit on behalf of United Federation of Teachers, *Camella Price et al. v. New York City Board of Education et al.*, Supreme Court of the State of New York, October 18, 2006.

2. The city administration compares cell phones to what dangerous instruments, according to a resolution cited in the viewpoint?

3. On what basis did the Department of Education reject a plan to construct lockers where cell phones could be stored, according to the author?

The UFT [United Federation of Teachers] represents more than 100,000 teachers and other educators who work in the City of New York's public schools ("Educators"). I respectfully make this affidavit in support of the UFT's motion for leave to appear in this action as *amicus curiae* [friend of the court] and, in that capacity, to present this Court with the unique perspective that Educators have on the issues raised herein.

As discussed in more detail below, cell phones are a lifeline for many parents and children. Indeed, one need look no further than the September 11 [2001] terrorist attacks, this month's [October 2006] [Cory] Lidle plane tragedy[1] or the Roosevelt Island tram incident [in which sixty-nine passengers were trapped for hours] to see their perceived importance in securing children's safety. At the same time, the use of cell phones inside classrooms and schools can be potentially disruptive and even dangerous. It is necessary, therefore, to find a balance that prohibits cell phone usage in school, but permits children to have them in traveling to and from school. Unlike most urban school systems that have crafted policies to achieve this balance, the [New York City] Department of Education (the "DOE") has instituted an outright ban on the possession of cell phones in schools. It has taken the position that, by doing so, it has facilitated the education of the "City's students in a safe and orderly environment in which teachers can de-

1. In October 2006, a plane carrying New York Yankees pitcher Cory Lidle and his flight instructor crashed into a high-rise building in Manhattan, killing them both and creating chaos.

vote their full energy to teaching . . . ," [according to the] Affidavit of Rose Albanese-DePinto. . . .

Not All Risky Items Can Be Banned

As the representative of teachers, the UFT is keenly aware that almost any item that a student could conceivably bring to school—including pens, pencils, and even paper—could potentially be used for mischief or harm. Yet, it would be counterproductive to ban every possible source of mischief from the educational environment. Instead, based on city-wide parameters that ban their use in schools, parents, teachers and administrators could work together to develop a school-by-school cell phone policy. If teachers, parents and students are involved in this school-by-school planning, all will have a stake in enforcing the rules that are agreed upon—enforcement that is necessary for any aspects of an effective discipline code.

Educators are skilled professionals that, *inter alia* [among other things], are initially responsible for the supervision of classrooms and the maintenance of discipline and safety therein. Accordingly, they have first-hand experience in what is necessary to create a sound educational environment and safe schools. It is Educators who must, in the first instance, deal with the whole array of concerns—from cheating to bullying to violence—that the DOE claims supports the cell phone ban. Because of the unique role that Educators play in the instruction of New York City's public school children, the UFT respectfully believes that its perspective will be of special assistance to the Court in this matter. . . .

The UFT has developed a special expertise with respect to school safety.

Thus . . . the UFT's Executive Board unanimously passed a resolution stating, in pertinent part:

Cellphones Can Save Students' Lives

My teen grandson was in his high school at 4 P.M., long after everyone had left the school, to get a drink from his locker before soccer practice. Seconds after he took a drink, he began feeling a reaction (he has peanut allergies), did not have his EpiPen [auto-injector to counter severe allergic reactions] with him and a passing student happened to have a cell phone for him to call for help. Luckily it had a happy ending. I do not believe in cellphones in schools but I think there should be exceptions for the school boards to think about.

Mary-Anne Secord, Toronto Star, *April 19, 2007.*

Use of Cell Phones in Schools Resolution

Whereas, the City Administration has ordered that students be prohibited from carrying cell phones to schools comparing them to guns, knives, and box cutters; and

Whereas, in an era when students often commute to schools by public transportation, this ban on cell phones has raised serious concerns among parents for the safety of their children; and

Whereas, this Administration pays lip service to empowering administration and staff to maintain orderly schools, but does not trust them to deal with incidents of cell phone abuse; be it

Resolved, that in lieu of banning the possession of student cell phones outright, each school develops and enforces a policy prohibiting cell phone use by students in a school building including escalating penalties on students who violate the school policy; and be it further

Resolved, that this policy be written into the safety plan.

A Wholesale Ban Is Unnecessary

City Council Member Bill de Blasio—a parent of school-aged children himself—joined me at a May 8, 2006 press conference in urging the Mayor and Chancellor to allow students to bring their cell phones to school, but ban their use inside the building. Said Council Member de Blasio:

> As a middle school parent, I know that cell phones are an important way for parents and students to communicate. . . . While cell phones can cause legitimate problems inside school, this is about safety, too. I want to help school-age families and educators strike a balance that ensures parents are empowered to take responsibility for their children's welfare. . . .

Such a balance is possible. Ostensibly, the purpose of the cell phone ban is to remove an item that "negatively impact[s] the learning environment"; is "a tool for cheating"; can be used for "taking and disseminating illicit photograph[s]"; makes it easier to "bully" others as well as eliminates a target for theft [see Respondents' Memorandum of Law in Support of Their Verified Answer ("Resp. Br."), DePinto Affidavit]. The UFT is keenly aware of the need to maintain discipline and order in classrooms and agrees that a ban on the *use* of cell phones in schools is necessary. This does not translate, however, into a rational basis for a wholesale prohibition on students bringing them into a school, which is tantamount to a ban on their possession. Far more narrow restrictions would achieve the DOE's stated purposes without endangering public school children's safety.

Ms. [Rose Albanese-]DePinto's affidavit provides a series of examples of how cell phones have been misused by individual students. In a school system of over 1,400 schools and 1.1 million students, while these examples provide a sound basis for a classroom prohibition, they do not provide the same for a wholesale ban on outright possession to and from schools. They serve instead to illustrate why empowering Educators and parents to develop an enforceable school-by-school cell phone policy is more appropriate. Indeed, in many schools, a policy requiring students to turn off their cell phones during class time or to keep their cell phones in their locker may be sufficient to prevent the overwhelming majority of instances of their misuse. Surely, a certain percentage of students can be expected to violate such a policy as they do the existing cell phone ban. In those situations, an outright ban on possession may be appropriate, but why hurt the thousands of parents and students who use the cell phones appropriately—only to and from school or in cases of emergency?

Consequences for Cheating and Crime

For example, without doubt a cell phone can be a tool for cheating and cheating is something we must crack down on. But does that mean we should ban any material that can be used for cheating—including pencils and pens? Because it is obviously impossible to learn in such an environment, the DOE, as with other aspects of the discipline code, must empower its staff to prevent cheating and impose consequences if cheating is discovered. Likewise, with respect to cell phones, the DOE must empower its staff and be willing to impose the consequences for a violation.

Similarly, cell phones may be the target of crime, but so too can almost anything of value. Indeed, the DOE does not ban from schools many other items that are worth a lot more money than cell phones. For example, sneakers in the style [*du jour*] can cost hundreds of dollars. Instead, it relies, as it must, on Educators, administrators and parents to provide a safe atmosphere for learning on a school-by-school basis.

A Proper Balance

The DOE argues that it declined to adopt a plan similar to Petitioners' proposal that it construct lockers so that students could check their phones as they enter a building because [as

stated in the DePinto affidavit] "the significant financial resources needed to design and build the facilities and thereafter
supervise and staff such an endeavor in 1,400 schools" are
better spent elsewhere. This misses the point. Whereas the
DOE makes a compelling case for why cell phones cannot be
used in classes, there are many schools that could craft a
policy that permits students to keep a cell phone on their person but require it [to] be turned off, allow students to keep a
cell phone in a school locker, or develop some other plan that
is appropriate for the individual school. Then, and only then,
in the few schools where there are persistent violations would
a discussion of an outright ban on possession be appropriate.
This would maintain the balance of keeping classrooms free
from disruption, yet permit students and parents [to] have the
perceived security that a cell phone provides.

> *"Supervision and monitoring is important for deterrence, detection, investigation, and responding to incidents of cyberbullying."*

Schools Should Enact Cyberbullying Policies

Nancy Willard

Nancy Willard, executive director of the Center for Safe and Responsible Use of the Internet, holds degrees in special education and law. In this viewpoint, she urges the implementation of school policies against cyberbullying—online cruelty or aggression—as well as cyberthreats, which are implied or direct threats to oneself or someone else. Cyberbullying can be constant, vicious, and have a dire impact on victims, she maintains. In consequence, school officials must work together, she contends, to establish policies for identifying, assessing, and punishing cyberbullying incidents and cyberthreats.

As you read, consider the following questions:

1. What example does Willard provide in support of her claim that some students become cyberbullies in response to their own victimization in school?

Nancy Willard, "An Educator's Guide to Cyberbullying and Cyberthreats: Responding to the Challenge of Online Social Aggression, Threats, and Distress," Center for Safe and Responsible Use of the Internet, April 2007. Copyright © 2005–2007 Nancy Willard. Reproduced by permission.

2. In the author's opinion, what are some effects of cyberbullying?
3. What are several ways in which school officials could respond to cyberbullying, in Willard's view?

Cyberbullying or cyberthreat material—text or images—may be posted on personal Web sites or blogs or transmitted via e-mail, discussion groups, message boards, chat, IM [instant messaging], or cell phones.

Students are engaging in this activity outside of school—but because the participants are also together in school, this off-campus activity may be impacting the school climate or interfering with the ability of students to be successful in school. Students are also engaging in this activity while using the district Internet system, while in school or when off-campus if access to the district Internet system is allowed, or when using personal digital devices, including cell phones, PDAs [personal digital assistants] or personal laptops, while on campus.

Types of Cyberbullying

A cyberbully may be a person whom the target knows or an online stranger. Or the cyberbully may be anonymous, so it is not possible to tell. A cyberbully may solicit involvement of other people who do not know the target—cyberbullying by proxy.

> Sue convinced Marilyn to post anonymous comments on a discussion board slamming Kelsey, a student she had gotten into a fight with. Marilyn was eager to win Sue's approval and fit into her group of friends, so she did as Sue requested.

Cyberbullying and cyberthreats may be related to in-school bullying. Sometimes, the student who is victimized at school is also being bullied online. But other times, the person who is victimized at school becomes a cyberbully and retaliates online. Still other times, the student who is victimized will share his or her anger or depression online as distressing material. When school officials respond to a report of cyberbullying or a cyberthreat, it is exceptionally important to take the time to fully investigate the situation—through an analysis of online as well as real-world interactions. Students should be held accountable for harmful material posted online, but punishing the student who is being victimized at school for responding to this victimization online will only increase the potential for additional harmful acts.

> *Eric is frequently bullied at school, but rarely responds. His social networking profile contains many angry, and sometimes threatening, comments directed at the students who torment him at school.*

Cyberbullying may involve relationships. If a relationship breaks up, one person may start to cyberbully the other person. Other times, teens may get into online fights about relationships.

> *Annie has been going out with Jacob, but is starting to have second thoughts about their relationship. As she is trying to back off, Jacob has become more controlling. He repeatedly sends her text messages, demanding to know where she is and whom she is with.*

Cyberbullying may be based on hate or bias—bullying others because of race, religion, physical appearance (including obesity), or sexual orientation.

> *Brad's blog is filled with racist profanity. Frequently, he targets black and Latino student leaders, as well as minority teachers, in his angry verbal assaults.*

Teens may think that cyberbullying is entertaining—a game to hurt other people.

> *Sitting around the computer with her friends, Judy asked, "Who can we mess with?" Judy started IM-ing with Brittany, asking her many personal questions. The next day, the girls were passing around Brittany's IM at school.*

Shocking Cyberharassment Statistics

- Seventeen percent of students surveyed in 2004 by my institution, the Rochester Institute of Technology, reported that they had been harassed online. Eight percent said they had been threatened; 6 percent had been cyberstalked; and another 6 percent had been victims of identity theft. One in three claimed to know the perpetrator prior to the crime. That shouldn't be surprising, given that the students also admitted to being offenders—especially in instances of pirating and academic dishonesty.

- One in three children ages 6 to 17 reported having been victimized online in a 2005 study on cyberbullying conducted by University of Wisconsin and Florida State University researchers. The respondents also reported feeling angry, sad, or depressed as a result, and often did not tell their parents about the incidents for fear of losing computer privileges.

- A 2006 national study of online youth victimization conducted by University of New Hampshire researchers found that one in seven reported receiving unwanted sexual solicitations. One in three received unwanted sexual material, and one in 11 experienced harassment, including threats.

Samuel C. McQuade III, "We Must Educate Young People About Cybercrime Before They Start College," Chronicle of Higher Education, *January 5, 2007.*

Impact of Cyberbullying

It is widely known that face-to-face bullying can result in long-term psychological harm to targets. This harm includes low self-esteem, depression, anger, school failure and avoidance, and, in some cases, school violence or suicide. It is possible that the harm caused by cyberbullying may be greater than harm caused by traditional bullying because . . .

- Online communications can be extremely vicious.

- There is no escape for those who are being cyberbullied—victimization is ongoing, 24/7.

- Cyberbullying material can be distributed worldwide and is often irretrievable.

- Cyberbullies can be anonymous and can solicit the involvement of unknown "friends."

- Teens may be reluctant to tell adults what is happening online or through their cell phones because they are emotionally traumatized, think it is their fault, fear greater retribution, or fear online activities or cell phone use will be restricted.

A group of girls at Alan's school had been taunting him through instant messaging, teasing him about his small size, daring him to do things he couldn't do, suggesting that the world would be a better place if he committed suicide. One day, he shot himself. His last online message was "Sometimes the only way to get the respect you deserve is to die." This is . . . a true story. . . .

Establishing a Policy

Addressing the concerns of cyberbullying and cyberthreats will require a systemic change. Most members of the safe school committee [a group of administrators, counselors, and safety officers] will have little understanding of how the district Internet system is managed and may have little insight into Internet technologies and activities. While some of the teacher or librarian members of the educational technology committee may have insight into safe schools issues, the technology staff may have much less insight. To manage the concerns of cyberbullying and cyberthreats, these two committees must work together, with the safe schools committee moving into a position of responsibility. . . .

The key components of an effective approach to manage student Internet use include the following.

It is necessary to increase the level of use for high-quality educational activities and decrease "Internet recess" activities. Educators know what happens during recess. This requires effective professional and curriculum development and specific expectations for teachers about the instructional use of technologies by students. The curriculum and instruction department should be responsible for coordinating educational technology-based instruction, not the technical services department.

The Internet use policy must be coordinated with disciplinary policies and address:

- Access to inappropriate material.

- Unacceptable communication and communication safety.

- Unlawful and inappropriate activities.

- Protection of student personal information.

- Notice of limited expectation of privacy.

- Requirement of reporting cyberbullying or threats.

Effective supervision and monitoring is important for deterrence, detection, investigation, and responding to incidents of cyberbullying and cyberthreats. Monitoring should be sufficient to establish the expectation among students that there is a high probability that instances of misuse will be detected and result in disciplinary action. An effective supervision approach for teachers to use [is to] frequently and randomly request to see the browser history file of individual students whenever students are using the Internet in class.

Technical monitoring of district Internet use that utilizes intelligent content analysis is recommended as the best approach. This kind of a technology monitors all traffic and reports on traffic that has elements that raise a "reasonable suspicion," thus allowing an administrator to review such reports. The technology works in accord with "search and seizure" standards. Another technical approach to monitoring allows for real-time remote viewing of any computer monitor in the building or computer lab.

Notice of the existence of monitoring will help to deter inappropriate activity. However it is important for students and staff to understand that no technology is perfect. Students should not rely on monitoring, but should report any concerns. . . .

Cyberbully Situation Review

School officials should establish a process to review situations involving cyberbullying incidents or cyberthreats. Review team members could include an administrator, counselor/psychologist, technology coordinator, librarian, school resource officer, and community mental health resource. However, for most incidents, this entire team will likely not be needed.

- *Imminent Threat.* If the online material appears to present a legitimate imminent threat of violence and danger to others school officials should contact law enforcement and initiate a protective response. But it is also necessary to continue with the following evidence gathering steps.

- *Evidence Gathering.* The evidence gathering should include preserving all evidence, and ensuring the identity of the cyberbully(ies), and may include searching for additional harmful material.

- *Violence or Suicide Assessment.* School officials should ask whether the evidence gathered raises concerns that student(s) may pose a risk of harm to others or self. Recognize that the threat of violence or suicide may come from student(s) who posted the material or from student(s) who were victimized.

- *Cyberbully Assessment.* An assessment must be made regarding whether the school can respond directly, with formal discipline by questioning whether there is a school nexus and substantial disruption or interference, or threat thereof. It is also necessary to gain a "root cause" understanding of the relationships and issues between the participants to determine whether harmful online material has been posted in retaliation for bullying.

Cyberbully Response Options

- *Formal Discipline.* School officials may be able to impose formal disciplinary response if a school nexus and substantial disruption has been established. But it is still necessary to address removal of materials, potential of continuation or retaliation by the student or online "buddies," and the support needs of the target.

- *Parent/Student/Staff Response Options.* Other response options, with or without formal discipline include:

- Calmly and strongly tell the cyberbully to stop.

- Ignore the cyberbully.

- File a complaint with the web site, Internet service provider or cell phone company.

- Have the parents of the target contact the cyberbully's parents or contact an attorney.

- Contact the police.

"Schools already have harassment policies in place and it would be unnecessary for the state legislature to pass redundant legislation."

School Cyberbullying Policies Are Not Needed

Carmine Boal

Carmine Boal is a Republican in the Iowa House of Representatives. In this viewpoint, she opposes legislation that mandates cyberbullying policies for schools in her state. They are unnecessary, she claims, because schools already have antiharassment policies. Furthermore, Boal points out, by denoting specific traits or characteristics upon which harassment may be based, the proposed legislation omits students whose characteristics are not specified. A better option, she proposes, is for parents, teachers, and administrators to work together to confront bullying and encourage respect.

As you read, consider the following questions:

1. In Boal's opinion, what model policy has been adopted by nearly all school districts?

Carmine Boal, "Boal Says 'Effective Teaching,' Not More Laws, Will Stop Bullies," *Des Moines Register*, February 16, 2007, p. 4. Reproduced by permission of the author.

2. What are five of the traits upon which harassment may be based, according to Boal's interpretation of the defeated bill?

3. In the author's view, what type of schools would not have been required to obey certain parts of the bill based on their religious tenets?

A bill passed by the Iowa House recently would require all schools to adopt a policy declaring harassment and bullying in schools as against school policy. It is a reasonable assumption no one condones the practice of harassment or bullying of any student for any reason at any time, and it seems most would favor its passage.

However, it is also my guess most people would assume schools already have harassment policies in place and it would be unnecessary for the state legislature to pass redundant legislation.

I assumed the same. Upon researching the question, I found that in order to be accredited by the State of Iowa, all public and non-public schools must have a student discipline policy addressing harassment per Iowa Administrative Code 281–12. Almost all school districts have adopted the model policy of the Iowa Association of School Boards, which closely mirrored the rule language.

Defining Harassment

So why should the legislature pass another law to mandate schools do something they have already done? The key is in how the bill defines harassment and bullying and the true intent of the passage of this legislation.

The bill defines harassment and bullying as "any conduct toward a student which is based on any actual or perceived trait or characteristic of the student and which creates an objectively hostile school environment." The bill then lists the traits or characteristics upon which harassment or bullying

Schools Must Allow Certain Online Speech

School officials need to be careful that they do not respond in a knee-jerk fashion and censor student speech simply because they don't like it or find it offensive. As Judge Rodney Sippel wrote in the *Beussink [v. Woodland R-IV School]* case [in which a student was suspended for criticizing his school on his personal Web page]: "Disliking or being upset by the content of a student's speech is not an acceptable justification for limiting student speech under *Tinker [v. Des Moines Independent School District]* [which found that speech can be censored if it might disrupt the school]."

"I do think schools want to be careful reacting to anything they don't like with disciplinary action because courts tend to be very skeptical of school actions based on opposition to the content of a student's expression," said Thomas Hutton with the National School Board Association. . . .

Schools must avoid an inflexible, zero-tolerance mindset. Some offensive student expression on the Internet merits First Amendment protection. Other material may cross the line into unprotected categories of speech, such as true threats, or expose a child to potential civil liability. This reality mandates that schools not take a knee-jerk, one-size-fits-all approach.

Davis L. Hudson Jr.,
Student Online Expression: What Do the Internet
and MySpace Mean for 'Students' First Amendment Rights?,
First Amendment Center, www.firstamendmentcenter.org.

can be based. The list includes age, color, creed, national origin, race, religion, marital status, sex, sexual orientation, gender identity, physical attributes, physical or mental ability or disability, ancestry, political party preference, political belief, socioeconomic status, or familial status.

Currently only three other states—California, New Jersey and Vermont—have a similar harassment and bullying law which lists specific characteristics on which harassment or bullying can be based.

A key amendment offered would have eliminated the list of traits or characteristics and instead included the word "all" to ensure the protection of all students from harassment and bullying. This amendment was not acceptable to the majority party and was defeated.

A More Effective Solution

One must ask why language that would protect all students from harassment and bullying would be less preferable to language that provides a list that may not include certain students. It seems to me that such a specific list could provide more headaches for schools to administer. Because taking the list out of the legislation was not negotiable, it became apparent there was an additional agenda for those who supported the bill other than protecting all students from bullying.

To their credit, the majority party did allow an amendment that would remove non-public schools from this requirement, recognizing that the inclusion of some of the traits might be in opposition to their religious tenets. They also agreed to include cyber bullying in the bill. While I am grateful for those concessions, I was still unable to vote for final passage of the bill.

The bottom line is no amount of words added to the Iowa Code will stop the age-old practice of bullying. Effectiveness is achieved when students, parents, teachers and administrators join together to confront bullying and harassment. We must all take responsibility to do our part to change hearts and minds to make Ankeny a place where all students and all people are respected.

| "Schools can help children get regular
exercise and can offer courses on health
maintenance, including proper diet."

Schools Should
Implement Policies to
Help Combat Obesity

Ron Haskins, Christina Paxson, and Elisabeth Donahue

Ron Haskins, Christina Paxson, and Elisabeth Donahue are editors of a Princeton University–Brookings Institution publication, The Future of Children. *In this viewpoint, excerpted from a* Future of Children *policy brief, they maintain that childhood obesity is a growing problem that schools must work to mitigate. They recommend that schools offer healthier food choices and promote physical activity. However, they caution, such efforts are often impeded by powerful food and beverage lobbyists who have interests in school vending machines and by legislation that diverts money from physical education programs.*

As you read, consider the following questions:

1. According to this viewpoint, why do child development experts feel it is so important to establish healthy actions during childhood?

2. In the authors' opinion, how does the regulation of federal lunches and breakfasts differ from that of à la carte items?

3. Why haven't more districts opposed vending machines in their schools, in the authors' opinion?

Until recently, most Americans regarded weight as a matter of personal choice. But as the number of obese children has tripled over the past three decades, that laissez-faire view of obesity has grown to seem quaint, if not dangerous. The latest volume of the journal *The Future of Children* makes clear why the problem of obesity has entered the public domain. The serious health risks of obesity, combined with rapidly rising obesity-related health care costs, warrant not only public attention but also public action and spending. . . .

Rates of obesity are rising especially fast among children. Under the law, children are judged incapable of making rational and fully informed choices. In terms used by economists, they are not "rational consumers." Moreover, a pervasive finding of research on child development is that actions taken in childhood have major impacts on adult status and behavior. Not only are obese children likely to grow up to be obese adults, but also eating and exercise habits established during childhood will importantly shape eating and exercise in adulthood. Moreover, as a recent report from the National Institute of Medicine shows, children's food preferences are strongly influenced by advertising—a policy area that offers ample precedent for government regulation. Although First Amendment issues lurk, the nation's several-decade-long experience with smoking demonstrates that a combination of government mandatory regulation and industry "voluntary" self-regulation can dramatically change the advertising climate for children and adults. Ronald McDonald, unless he changes his supersizing ways, should be headed toward Joe Camel oblivion.

Why Focus on Schools?

Taken together, [obesity's serious health risks and rising health care costs] provide ample justification for government intervention to reduce childhood obesity. A host of policies and programs at the federal, state, and local level have been developed over the past decade or so to fight childhood obesity, and new programs and policies are certain to be developed in the years ahead. The new *Future of Children* volume devoted to obesity notes that these policies fall into four groups: prevention measures addressed to both children and parents; reduction of children's exposure to advertising of foods high in sugar and fat; improved delivery by pediatricians of preventive care and treatment for obesity and related medical conditions; and improved nutrition and physical activity within the schools. We believe that policies and programs implemented in the public schools hold the greatest promise.

Children spend a large part of their lives in school. They begin attending school at age five—and in many cases, especially with children from low-income families, at age four or even three—and most remain there until age eighteen. Nearly every school in the nation serves at least one and often two meals a day, five days a week. over all these years. Schools have the opportunity, then, both to influence the nutrition children receive on a regular basis and to help children establish healthful lifelong eating habits. In addition, schools can help children get regular exercise and can offer courses on health maintenance, including proper diet and exercise. Because schools also have frequent contact with parents, they may be able to influence both the foods children consume at home and their parents' understanding of the importance of physical activity for their children's health. In short, schools offer a prime target for those like us who want to reduce rates of obesity and thereby promote child health.

Changing the Menu

Foods available in schools fall into three categories: the federal school lunch and breakfast programs, à la carte food items available in the school cafeteria, and foods available in vending machines and other venues outside the school cafeteria. Because the à la carte items and vending machines compete with school meals, they are often collectively referred to as competitive foods. Foods in these three categories, however, are subject to very different rules.

The federal lunch and breakfast programs are highly regulated by the U.S. Department of Agriculture (USDA). These meals are gradually becoming more nutritious, if not (by student report) exactly delicious. By contrast, the à la carte items—thanks in part to the food companies that lobby Congress in Washington—are only loosely regulated by the federal government. The items offered à la carte vary widely from school to school, but foods high in fat and sugar like chips and cookies are usually available. Some schools even allow fast-food vendors such as Taco Bell, Subway, Domino's, and Pizza Hut to market their products in the school cafeteria.

As part of its modest efforts to control consumption of unhealthful foods at school, the federal government has labeled certain foods, including soda pop, water ices, chewing gum, and some candies, as being of "minimal nutritional value" and has ruled that they cannot be sold in the cafeteria during school meals. But many types of candy and other unhealthful foods have escaped that label and are free to compete directly with school meals in the cafeteria during lunch hour. And schools can make even foods of minimal nutritional value available outside the cafeteria during lunch time and throughout the day, especially in vending machines.

Congress has on several occasions modified the school lunch and breakfast programs, which were reauthorized in 2004 as part of an omnibus child nutrition law, to require schools to make meals more attractive and nutritious. To some extent, Congress, USDA, and local school authorities have worked together to improve school meals. A study commissioned by USDA showed that during the 1991–92 school year, lunches in nearly every school served by the school lunch program failed to meet accepted guidelines for fat and saturated fats. In response, USDA promulgated new standards to help school food service personnel reduce the fat content of meals and serve more nutritious food. A follow-up USDA study, based on survey data for 1994–96, found that although most schools still failed to meet the guidelines, the fat content of school meals had declined substantially, proving that administrative action by the federal government can directly affect the food consumed in the nation's schools.

Obstacles to Tough Federal Standards

For the past several years, Congress has been attentive to the obesity issue, although differences in political philosophy between Republicans and Democrats, together with the influence of the food lobby, have prevented any comprehensive initiatives. The debate over reauthorizing the child nutrition programs in 2004 illustrates the difficulty of using federal policy to require schools to provide more nutritious foods and reduce availability of unhealthful foods. Consider vending machines. Until recently, the content of vending machines, which are found in most school buildings, was mostly junk—candy, gum, and sodas. Many Democrats in Congress want to simply remove vending machines from the schools. That approach— mandating states and localities to take certain actions—is a regular feature of federal programs. Although Washington generally lacks the constitutional authority to require local schools to adopt specific educational policies, it does have the authority to require states and localities to adopt federal rules in exchange for federal dollars. Because local education agencies get well over $7 billion in federal aid a year to run their food programs, there is little doubt that the federal government could rule schools with vending machines ineligible to receive federal dollars for their school lunch or breakfast programs. If Congress or the Department of Agriculture enacted such a rule, vending machines would instantly disappear from almost every school in the nation. Reducing school vending would lead directly to improved child nutrition and health.

So why didn't Congress take this action during the 2004 reauthorization debate? While the debate over vending machines is largely a money issue at the local level, at the federal level it is really about federalism, with the debate playing out along party lines. Republicans, who control both the House and the Senate, are generally less supportive of mandates on states and localities than are Democrats. In addition, powerful lobbying groups for the food and beverage industry, led by companies such as Kraft and General Mills, as well as the Food Manufacturers Association, which represents a host of major food and beverage companies in Washington, have consistently opposed removing vending machines. The political philosophy of the majority party and the efforts of powerful lobbying groups are a lot to overcome.

Thus, after much debate, especially in the Senate, the parties reached a compromise: the 2004 child nutrition law required all local education agencies to develop a "wellness policy" that spelled out goals for nutrition and exercise and included guidelines for all foods sold in the schools. Merely requiring local schools to develop policies of a particular sort is by no means strong federal action, particularly since additional funding did not accompany the requirement, but it may have modest effects on some school districts because they must now give parents and other citizens an opportunity to help formulate nutrition goals and practices. Although as authors we are split on whether the federal government should require schools to remove vending machines that feature junk food, we agree that junk food has no place in schools and we can see the benefit of having state and local school authorities

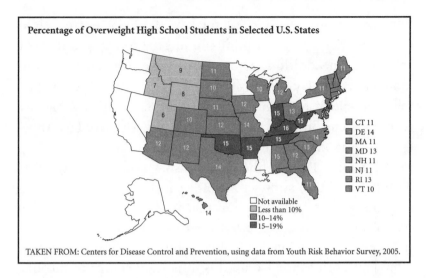

Percentage of Overweight High School Students in Selected U.S. States

CT 11
DE 14
MA 11
MD 13
NH 11
NJ 11
RI 13
VT 10

☐ Not available
☐ Less than 10%
■ 10–14%
■ 15–19%

TAKEN FROM: Centers for Disease Control and Prevention, using data from Youth Risk Behavior Survey, 2005.

take the initiative to improve the foods served to children during school hours. We believe state and local authorities should either remove vending machines or replace foods and beverages high in sugar and fat with more healthful foods and beverages such as fruit and juices.

Although vending machines survived federal efforts to remove them, the 2004 child nutrition debate showed that Congress is aware of the growing obesity problem and is willing to take at least modest action. In addition to the wellness policy requirement, the new law also contained incentives for schools to purchase fresh fruits and vegetables from local farmers and to serve more fresh salads and whole grain breads. The use of incentives rather than mandates shows yet again that Congress is reluctant to force schools to make major changes in their child nutrition policies and programs.

Schools Take Action

Given the reluctance of the federal government to move too quickly by using mandates, it is worth noting that many states and local school districts have now adopted tougher standards than those promulgated by Washington—actions that are not impeded in any way by federal law. By 2005, twenty-eight states had taken steps to limit commercial foods sold in their cafeterias. In addition, a few states have enacted laws, and more states are considering legislation, to restrict the vending machine sale of foods high in sugar and fat. Similarly, big city school systems in New York, Philadelphia, Chicago, Los Angeles, and elsewhere have taken strong action to limit vending machine sales. Perhaps the main reason more school districts have failed to take stronger action against vending machines is that the profits from vending machine sales go to the local school and are used to pay for extra-curricular, and sometimes even instructional, activities. Thus, it is difficult for local school authorities to give up this important source of income. Even so, evidence is now emerging that schools that have stressed more healthful foods such as milk, juices, and fruit in both their vending machines and their à la carte cafeteria menus have done so without losing revenue. In any case, states and local school districts that are restricting sales of foods and beverages high in fat and sugar are moving in the right direction. It would be unwise for school districts and child advocates to wait for the federal government to take stronger action. State and local policies can and should move even faster and further to ensure that schools serve more nourishing foods in the cafeteria and replace junk food with more healthful fare.

Increasing Physical Activity

Obesity prevention is a two-term proposition. Amount and type of food consumed is one term, and probably the most important. But the second term is exercise. The average American readily understands the problem. Indeed, that same average American is more than likely a victim of the many forces that conspire to turn both adults and children into couch potatoes. Cars and buses—especially school buses—have replaced legs as the way to get to work or school, depriving millions of Americans of a prime source of daily exercise. For inner-city residents, the threat of crime and random violence is a constant presence, forcing many to abandon parks, playgrounds, and other sources of play and exercise. And, of course, children are avid TV watchers. With one of the few proven antidotes to addictive TV watching being addictive electronic game playing, children now average about 3.5 hours a day of "screen" time. Both forms of electronic activity are triple-whammies in favor of obesity. Not only is the fixation on electronic amusements usually incompatible with physical activity, but also both TV and electronic games feature advertisements for foods loaded with sugar and fat, and children often snack while watching or playing.

Ironically, schools' commitment to providing physical activity for students has begun to suffer because of national concern with the mediocre (or worse) school achievement of U.S. students. No Child Left Behind, with its emphasis on academic standards and testing, has increased pressures on local schools to focus their attention on academic subjects and to divert money needed to support gym and other opportunities for physical activities. Academic excellence, however, should not be purchased at the price of regular exercise.

Suggested Actions from Recess to PE

Schools can take a host of actions to promote physical activity. Recess for elementary school children, required daily physical education (PE) classes for all children in grades 1 through 12, and a full menu of extracurricular sports and physical activity clubs should be high on the agenda for all local school systems. Nationally only a third of adolescents are physically active in PE classes for more than twenty minutes for three or more days each week, and nearly a third of elementary schools do not schedule recess on a regular basis. Contrast this record with the recommendation by the National Institute of Medicine that students have a minimum of thirty minutes a day of physical activity.

The issue for local school authorities involves priorities. Recess provides a prime example. The main ingredient necessary for daily recess for students through at least sixth grade is time. True, local school systems are spending more time on basic instruction in reading and mathematics than they did just a few years ago, but several hours still remain in the school day after even the most intense focus on basic education. A school system with the will to emphasize exercise for its elementary schools can find time for at least thirty minutes of recess each day. Similarly, middle and high schools can require all students to take PE classes that involve strenuous physical activity five days a week, although this requirement will also necessitate additional spending. Our argument is that given the breadth and depth of the obesity problem, the commitment to regular physical exercise should be high on the priority list for every public school system. Even without new funding, local systems can move resources from other activities to ensure regular physical activity by all their students at every grade level. . . .

Schools can affect the food children consume during the day and perhaps even shape their food preferences as they mature and develop. Similarly, schools can have a direct effect on children's daily exercise. Schools, and to a lesser extent the federal government, have already taken important steps to improve nutrition and increase exercise. Children and society will benefit if schools push more aggressively in the direction they are already moving.

> "Each year approximately 800 school-
> aged children are killed in motor ve-
> hicle crashes during normal school
> travel hours."

Schools Should Make Accommodations for Safer Student Travel

Deb Moore

School districts should employ measures to keep students safe on their routes to and from school, according to Deb Moore in this viewpoint. She laments that a disproportionate number of teen drivers, bicyclists, and pedestrians suffer injuries or are killed during normal school travel hours as compared to other times of the day. In response, she proposes, school districts can limit student driving privileges, designate more crossing zones, install more stop signs, and segregate different types of traffic. Moore is the executive editor and publisher of the magazine School Planning & Management.

As you read, consider the following questions:

1. In Moore's view, how many school-aged children are non-fatally injured each year during normal school travel hours?

Deb Moore, "Kids and Cars," *School Planning & Management*, November 2004, p. 8. Reproduced by permission.

2. In what ways can school districts modify student driving policies, according to the author?

3. Where does the author suggest locating driveways and parent parking in schools?

The November issue of SP&M [*School Planning & Management*] is always a special one that focuses on making our schools safer places for kids. The concern about 'school safety' conjures up images of terrorism and homicides, theft and vandalism, drug and alcohol use, and bullying. Reports show that students age 12 to 18 were victims of about two million nonfatal crimes of violence or theft at school in 2001. The data on homicides and suicides at school show there were 32 school-associated violent deaths in the United States between July 1, 1999 and June 30, 2000, including 24 homicides—16 of which involved school-aged children. To combat these problems, schools and communities are devising safety plans and installing safety technologies, but what are we doing to make the trip to school safer?

Motor Vehicle Crashes Involving Youths

According to Transportation Research Board Special Report 269, *The Relative Risks of School Travel: A National Perspective and Guidance for Local Community Risk Assessment*, "each year approximately 800 school-aged children are killed in motor vehicle crashes during normal school travel hours. This figure represents about 14 percent of the 5,600 child deaths that occur annually on U.S. roadways and two percent of the nation's yearly total of 40,000 motor vehicle deaths. Of these 800 deaths, about 20 (two percent)—five school bus passengers and 15 pedestrians—are school bus related. The other 98 percent of school-aged deaths occur in passenger vehicles or to pedestrians, bicyclists or motorcyclists. A disproportionate share of these passenger vehicle-related deaths (approximately 450 of the 800 deaths or 55 percent) occur when a teenager is

Traffic Accidents During School Hours

According to Washington State Department of Transportation data, most teenage driver collisions occur in October, November, and December. Most commonly, accidents happen on Fridays. The most common hours of the day for teenage collision is from 2–6 p.m. and secondarily from 7–8 in the morning. Not coincidentally, these are the hours before and after school and the times when a teenage driver is more likely to have teenage passengers in the car. . . .

A study of three counties in North Carolina found that there was a higher rate of teenagers' motor vehicle crashes during the lunch hours in the two counties with open-campus lunch policies compared with the county without. It was noted that the students from the counties with open-campus lunch schools were carrying more passengers with them when they were involved in lunch-hour crashes. Open campus lunch policies expose teenagers to additional driving time and encourage conditions in which multiple teens ride together, a known risk factor for crashes involving teen drivers.

René Ewing & Associates, LLC,
Teenage Driving Study, *January 2007.*

driving. At the same time, approximately 152,000 school-age children are nonfatally injured during normal school travel hours each year. More than 80 percent (about 130,000) of these nonfatal injuries occur in passenger vehicles: only four percent (about 6,000) are school bus related (about 5,500 school bus passengers and 500 school bus pedestrians), 11 percent (about 16,500) occur to pedestrians and bicyclists, and fewer than one percent (500) are to passengers in other buses."

There are many modes of transportation used by students in their daily trek to and from school ranging from walking or biking, to a ride from mom/dad, to public transportation or the yellow school bus. For many high school students, the method of choice is their own car. Many factors play a part when determining safety/risk including the mode of transportation, the use of safety equipment, infrastructure design and student behavior. When looking just at mode of transportation and calculating the risk, traveling to school or school-related activities by school bus, public transportation and passenger vehicles with adult drivers have injury estimates and fatality counts below those expected, based on exposure to risk as implied by the number of trips taken and student miles traveled. On the other hand, passenger vehicles with teen drivers, bicycling and walking have estimated injury rates and fatality counts disproportionate to exposure.

Steps Districts Can Take to Protect Students

While they can't control the highways, districts can change their policies regarding student driving privileges by limiting available parking or closing the campus during school hours, thereby eliminating carloads of kids going off campus for lunch. Modifications could also be made to minimum walking distance, especially in cases were there is not adequate infrastructure for walking or biking. Early and late buses could be made available for students participating in after-school activities. Working with the community and local government agencies, schools can make access to the site safer, ensuring that sites are marked with signage that designates school zones and crossing zones, keeping off-site sidewalks maintained and installing stop signs or red lights where necessary.

Good site design can reduce situations in which motor vehicles, pedestrians and bicyclists conflict with one another. Student loading areas should be segregated from traffic and pedestrian walkways. Buses and parent parking should be kept separate, mixing types of traffic can cause confusion and accidents. Traffic should be one way with clearly marked entrances and exits. Adequate sidewalks and crosswalks should be provided for students, employees and visitors to the school building, the playgrounds and the athletic fields. Driveways and parent parking should be near the main entrance and administration offices, as well as the auditorium, cafeteria and athletic fields. Playgrounds for elementary students should be kept separate from parking lots and traffic areas.

Lack of Funds Is No Excuse

Like many other things in school, it all comes down to resources. Are there funds available to purchase a site large enough to adequately handle traffic? Are there funds available to maintain the walkways, bike paths and crosswalks? Are there funds available to offer early and late bus services? When 800 school-aged children are killed and 152,000 are nonfatally injured traveling back and forth to school each year, can we afford to blame it on lack of funds?

Periodical Bibliography

The following articles have been selected to supplement the diverse views presented in this chapter.

Associated Press — "School Cell Phone Ban Causes Uproar," May 12, 2006.

Andy Carvin — "New Federal Legislation Would Ban Online Social Networks in Schools & Libraries," PBS Teachers learning.now, May 11, 2006. www.pbs.org.

Michael Fitzpatrick — "Deleting Online Predators Act of 2006," H.R. 5319, May 9, 2006. www.govtrack.us.

Forsite Group — "MySpace: Safeguard Your Students, Protect Your Network," 8e6 Technologies, 2006. www.8e6.com.

Declan McCullagh — "Lawmakers Take Aim at Social-Networking Sites," CNET News.com, May 10, 2006.

Samuel C. McQuade III — "We Must Educate Young People About Cyber-crime Before They Start College," *Chronicle of Higher Education*, January 5, 2007.

National School Boards Association — *Leadership Insider*, August 2006. www.nsba.org.

National Public Radio — "How Far Should Schools Go to Fight Obesity?" *Talk of the Nation*, April 24, 2007. www.npr.org.

National School Safety and Security Services — "School Safety Issues Related to the Terrorist Attacks on the United States," 2007. www.schoolsecurity.org.

Kevin Poulsen — "Scenes from the MySpace Backlash," *Wired*, February 27, 2006.

Julie Sturgeon — "Bullies in Cyberspace," *District Administration*, September 2006.

For Further Discussion

Chapter 1

1. The mission of the Office of National Drug Control Policy is to establish priorities and objectives to reduce illicit drug use and sales in U.S. The National Organization for the Reform of Marijuana Laws, by contrast, works to support and legalize the responsible use of marijuana by adults. How are these organizations' goals coloring their opinions on the use of random drug testing in schools?

2. Reread the viewpoints by Gerald N. Tirozzi, et al. Do you think zero tolerance codes deter misbehavior and ensure consistent discipline among students? Use facts from the viewpoints to bolster your assertions.

3. The Christian Law Association asserts that teaching alternate theories to evolution is good science and is a necessary part of students' education. However, *amici curiae*, or friends of the court, in *Selman v. Cobb County* believe that teaching that evolution is merely a theory encourages unscientific thinking among students and undermines their science education. With which author do you agree, and why?

Chapter 2

1. After reading Viewpoints 1 and 2, do you think metal detectors should be used in schools, and under what circumstances, if any? Why or why not?

2. Rebecca Sausner states that the perceived need for increased school surveillance has trumped privacy concerns. How do you think Ronnie Casella would respond to this claim? Explain.

3. In your opinion, what are the best methods for keeping schools safe? What are their advantages and drawbacks? Refer to the viewpoints for information to support your answer.

Chapter 3

1. *Northwest Florida Daily News*, Kent J. Fetzer, and Mike Kelly use varying styles of argument to make their points regarding school uniforms and the right to expression. Assess each style and identify which one you find most convincing. Support your answer.

2. Peter H. Schuck argues that disabled students are rarely suspended or expelled for misbehaving in school. Yet Russell Skiba and his co-researchers claim in their viewpoint in Chapter 1 that disabled students are disciplined more often than other students. With which author do you agree? Explain why.

3. The American Civil Liberties Union uses court cases to bolster its argument that students should be allowed to form gay/straight alliances in schools. Linda P. Harvey, by contrast, refers to opinion polls, white papers, and resources from gay rights organizations in her viewpoint. Which author makes the most effective use of evidence, in your opinion? Why?

Chapter 4

1. Whereas Armstrong Williams claims that cell phones should be banned in schools because they are disruptive, Randi Weingarten contends that they should be allowed for safety reasons. With which viewpoint do you agree, and why?

2. After reading Viewpoints 3 and 4, do you think cyberbullying is an issue that schools should address, and if not, whose responsibility should it be? Support your answer.

3. Deb Moore sets forth several recommendations for safer student travel. Assess three of her suggestions and explain why you do or do not believe each should be implemented.

Organizations to Contact

The editors have compiled the following list of organizations concerned with the issues debated in this book. The descriptions are derived from materials provided by the organizations. All have publications or information available for interested readers. The list was compiled on the date of publication of the present volume; names, addresses, phone and fax numbers, and e-mail and Internet addresses may change. Be aware that many organizations take several weeks or longer to respond to inquiries, so allow as much time as possible.

ABA Juvenile Justice Center
740 Fifteenth St. NW, Seventh Floor, Washington, DC   20005
(202) 662-1506 • fax: (202) 662-1507
e-mail: juvjus@abanet.org
Web site: www.abanet.org/child/juvenile-justice.shtml

Part of the American Bar Association, the Juvenile Justice Center disseminates information on juvenile justice systems and laws that pertain to youths. The center provides leadership to state and local practitioners, judges, youth workers, and policy makers. Although its interests include prevention of school violence, the center opposes zero tolerance policies. Among its publications is the quarterly *Children's Legal Rights Journal*.

American Civil Liberties Union (ACLU)
125 Broad St., Eighteenth Floor, New York, NY   10004-2400
(212) 549-2500
e-mail: aclu@aclu.org
Web site: www.aclu.org

Through litigation, education, and advocacy, the ACLU works to defend Americans' civil rights guaranteed by the U.S. Constitution. Seeking to protect the rights of students and others, it opposes random school searches, suspicionless drug testing,

216

zero tolerance policies, and other measures that may abridge personal freedoms. The ACLU offers policy statements, pamphlets, the *Student Organizing Manual*, and the semiannual newsletter *Civil Liberties Alert*.

American Library Association (ALA)
50 E. Huron St., Chicago, Illinois 60611
(800) 545-2433
e-mail: library@ala.org
Web site: www.ala.org

As the oldest and largest library association in the world, the ALA aims to ensure high-quality library and information services accessible to all of the public. Because it works to promote intellectual freedom and the open flow of information, the ALA opposes mandatory Internet filters and book censorship in schools. Its Web site contains a section on censorship in school, information about ALA's Banned Books Week, articles, reports, and books that the ALA publishes.

Cato Institute
1000 Massachusetts Ave. NW, Washington, DC 20001-5403
(202) 842-0200 • fax: (202) 842-3490
Web site: www.cato.org

The Cato Institute, a libertarian public policy research foundation, is dedicated to limiting the role of government and protecting individual liberties. Some of the many topics it discusses are affirmative action in college admissions, Internet censorship, and abuse and inefficiency in America's schools. The institute produces the quarterly magazine *Regulation*, the bimonthly *Cato Policy Report*, *Cato Journal* three times a year, a monthly audio CD, numerous books, and various policy papers, such as "Why We Fight: How Public Schools Cause Social Conflict."

Center for the Prevention of School Violence (CPSV)
1801 Mail Service Center, Raleigh, NC 27699-1801
(800) 299-6054

e-mail: megan.q.howell@ncmail.net
Web site: www.cpsv.org

As part of the North Carolina Department of Juvenile Justice and Delinquency Prevention, the CPSV is a primary point of contact for information, programs, and research about school violence. As a clearinghouse, it provides information about all aspects of the problem of school violence as well as possible strategies to promote safer schools and foster the positive development of youths. *School Resource Officers: What We Know, What We Think We Know, What We Need to Know* is one of its reports.

Education World
1062 Barnes Rd., Suite 205, Wallingford, CT   06492
e-mail: webmaster@educationworld.com
Web site: www.educationworld.com

At the Education World Web site, teachers and administrators share ideas, find lesson plans and materials, ask questions, and read daily columns to help them in their mission to provide high-quality education to students. Educators can browse hundreds of articles written by experts covering topics such as dress codes and school safety. The site distributes *Education World Newsletter* and *Administrator's Desk Newsletter* weekly.

Family Research Council (FRC)
801 G St. NW, Washington, DC   20001
(202) 393-2100 • fax: (202) 393-2134
Web site: www.frc.org

Through promotion of Judeo-Christian values, the council seeks to protect the interests of the traditional family, the institution of marriage, and parental autonomy and responsibility. FRC supports abstinence education, the teaching of intelligent design in schools, and school prayer; it opposes what it calls homosexual advocacy in schools. On its Web site it makes available its fact papers, commentary, and reports, including "Ten Ways to Pray in Public Schools."

National Association of Elementary School Principals (NAESP)

1615 Duke St., Alexandria, VA 22314
(800) 386-2377 • fax: (800) 396-2377
e-mail: naesp@naesp.org
Web site: www.naesp.org

Founded in 1921, NAESP provides support for elementary and middle school principals and administrators. It offers resources such as articles, sample school policies drafts, and studies on various issues ranging from school uniforms to student discipline to online safety. Among the publications it distributes are *Principal Magazine*, the monthly newsletter *Communicator*, the bimonthly e-newsletter *Before The Bell*, and the quarterly e-newsletter *Research Roundup*.

National Education Association (NEA)

1201 Sixteenth St. NW, Washington, DC 20036
(202) 883-8400 • fax: (202) 822-7974
Web site: www.nea.org

NEA is America's oldest and largest volunteer-based organization dedicated to advancing the cause of public education. Its commitments at the local, state, and national levels include conducting workshops for teachers, lobbying for needed school resources and higher educational standards, and spearheading innovative projects that reshape the learning process. Two of NEA's publications are the monthly magazine *NEA Today Online* and the biannual report *Thoughts and Action*.

Student Drug-Testing Coalition

e-mail: mattf@rrohio.com
Web site: www.studentdrugtesting.org

Composed of parents and members of drug prevention groups, the Student Drug-Testing Coalition aims to help students improve their future by keeping them—and their schools—free of drugs. It provides information and resources for schools to implement non-punitive drug testing programs to prevent addiction as well as accidents and crimes related to addiction. The booklet *Model Legislation For Student Drug Testing Programs: State Bill and Insertion Language* is available on the site, as well as statistics, case studies, and commentary about student drug testing.

Bibliography of Books

Kern Alexander — *The Law of Schools, Students and Teachers in a Nutshell.* St. Paul, MN: West Group, July 2003.

Anti-Defamation League — *Responding to Bigotry and Intergroup Strife on Campus.* New York: Anti-Defamation League, 2001.

Rami Benbenishty and Ron Avi Astor — *School Violence in Context: Culture, Neighborhood, Family, School, and Gender.* New York: Oxford University Press, 2005.

William C. Bosher Jr. et al. — *The School Law Handbook: What Every Leader Needs to Know.* Alexandria, VA: Association for Supervision and Curriculum Development, 2004.

Susan Brooks-Young — *Critical Technology Issues for School Leaders.* Thousand Oaks, CA: Corwin, 2006.

David L. Brunsma — *The School Uniform Movement and What It Tells Us About American Education.* Lanham, MD: Rowman & Littlefield Education, 2004.

Ronnie Casella — *Selling Us the Fortress: The Promotion of Techno-Security Equipment for Schools.* New York: Routledge, 2006.

Bruce S. Cooper et al. — *Better Policies, Better Schools: Theories and Applications.* Boston: Allyn & Bacon, 2003.

Joan Del Fattore

The Fourth R: Conflicts Over Religion in America's Public Schools. New Haven, CT: Yale University Press, 2005.

Michael Dorn and Chris Dorn

Innocent Targets: When Terrorism Comes to School. Macon, GA: Safe Havens International, 2005.

Laura Finley and Peter Finley

Piss Off!: How Drug Testing and Other Privacy Violations Are Alienating America's Youth. Monroe, ME: Common Courage, 2004.

Patricia H. Hinchey

Student Rights: A Reference Handbook. Santa Barbara, CA: ABC-CLIO, 2001.

Ian K. Macgillivray

Sexual Orientation and School Policy: A Practical Guide for Teachers, Administrators, and Community Activists. Lanham, MD: Rowman & Littlefield, 2003.

Erica R. Meiners

Right to Be Hostile: Schools, Prisons, and the Making of Public Enemies. New York: Routledge, 2007.

Katherine S. Newman et al.

Rampage: The Social Roots of School Shootings. New York: Basic Books, 2004.

Jamin B. Raskin

We the Students: Supreme Court Cases for and About Students. Washington, DC: CQ, 2003.

Charles Russo et al.   *The Educational Rights of Students: International Perspectives on Demystifying the Legal Issues.* Lanham, MD: Rowman & Littlefield Education, 2006.

Winn Schwartau   *Internet & Computer Ethics for Kids (and Parents & Teachers Who Haven't Got a Clue).* Seminole, FL: Interpact, 2001.

James T. Sears, ed.   *Gay, Lesbian, and Transgender Issues in Education: Programs, Policies, and Practice.* New York: Harrington Park, 2005.

Russell J. Skiba and Gil G. Noam   *Zero Tolerance: Can Suspension and Expulsion Keep Schools Safe?* San Francisco: Jossey-Bass, 2002.

Harvey Silverglate and Josh Gewolb   *FIRE's Guide to Due Process and Fair Procedure on Campus.* Philadelphia: Foundation for Individual Rights in Education, 2004.

May Taylor and Ethel Quayle   *Child Pornography: An Internet Crime.* New York: Brunner-Routledge, 2003.

R. Murray Thomas   *God in the Classroom: Religion and America's Public Schools.* Westport, CT: Praeger, 2007.

Dick Thornburgh and Herbert S. Lin, eds.   *Youth, Pornography, and the Internet.* Washington, DC: National Academy, 2002.

Nancy E. Willard   *Computer Ethics, Etiquette, and Safety for the 21st-Century Student.* Eugene, OR: International Society for Technology in Education, 2002.

Index